THE POCKET GUIDE TO
ANTIQUES
& COLLECTABLES

THE POCKET GUIDE TO
ANTIQUES

&COLLECTABLES

A Marshall Edition
Conceived, edited and designed by
Marshall Editions Ltd
The Orangery
161 New Bond Street
London W1Y 9PA

First published in the UK as four volumes in 1995 by
BBC Books, a division of BBC Enterprises Ltd, Woodlands,
80 Wood Lane, London W12 0TT

This edition first published in the UK in 1999 by
Marshall Publishing Ltd

ISBN 1-84028-230-4

10 9 8 7 6 5 4 3 2 1

EDITORS GWEN RIGBY, HEATHER MAGRILL
ART EDITOR HELEN SPENCER
PICTURE EDITOR ELIZABETH LOVING
ASSISTANT EDITOR SIMON BEECROFT
ART DIRECTOR JOHN BIGG

ILLUSTRATIONS by János Márffy,
Stan North, Coral Mula
ALL PHOTOGRAPHS by Clive Corless,
except the following:
CHRISTIE'S IMAGES: 46; 48c; 63; 67r
COURTESY, WINTERTHUR MUSEUM: 48b.
r = right, b = bottom, c = centre

Valuation is an imprecise art and prices vary for
many reasons. The valuations given are estimated
auction prices at the time of going to press.
As auctions take place in the public arena, this
is considered to be the fairest value.

Antiques Roadshow is a trademark of the British Broadcasting
Corporation and is used under licence.

Origination 1995 editions by Master Image, Singapore
Origination 1999 editions by HBM Print Ltd, Singapore
Printed and bound in Portugal by Printer Portuguesa

CONTENTS

INTRODUCTION

Learning to spot the real thing and understanding style are all part of the excitement of collecting antiques. Whether you are a collector needing to know how much you might expect to pay for a specific item, a junk shop browser or even just an armchair devotee, *The Pocket Guide to Antiques and Collectables* will prove an ideal reference source.

The book is divided into four sections: small and decorative furniture; pottery and porcelain; dolls, toys and games; and clocks and watches.

Each section is written by a well-known expert from the BBC's Antiques Roadshow.

In the small furniture section, John Bly examines all the major items of household furniture, from chairs and desks to wine coolers and dumb waiters.

David Battie offers a range of pottery and porcelain, from commemorative jugs and mugs to chamber pots and dressing table sets, while Hilary Kay explores the market for toys and games.

Simon Bull brings together all manner of timepieces from longcase and carriage clocks to fob and wrist watches.

Each section is subdivided into different areas. Each of these provides a background history to the topic – when and where production started, how the item was made and what it was used for. Where relevant, details of style are highlighted with tips on how to recognize an authentic item.

Each entry is illustrated by a colour photograph and described in detail together with a price guide. Unless you are a serious collector and know you can sell an item on, it is important to bear in mind, when thinking about buying, whether you actually like the object or not.

Above all, buying collectables should be fun and affordable. Do not buy something simply with an eye to a profit unless you are really sure of yourself. Ultimately, an item is only worth what someone else will pay for it. Although the price guides in this book are an indication of what you might expect to pay for an item, it does not necessarily follow that you will be able to sell it on for more, or, depending on the fluctuations in the market place, that you would receive the same price you paid for it.

In all areas, the condition of an object will increase its value. If it is one of a set, the set will be worth more than the sum of its individual parts. Items that have undergone non-professional repair may be worth less in their repaired state than they would have been had they been left alone. Keeping this in mind, don't repair any items in your collection yourself – take damaged pieces to a reputable restorer who is a specialist in the type of object that you have. The importance of insuring valuable items against theft or damage is also discussed in the book.

Whatever you buy, be it for pleasure or profit, the section on care will help you to maintain the condition and value of your items. A checklist provides a list of tips for the buyer, indicating what you should look for and the vital questions you should ask. Collections of interest are also included – remember, looking at these are the best way to improve your knowledge and familiarity.

SMALL & DECORATIVE FURNITURE

SMALL & DECORATIVE FURNITURE

THIS SECTION IS AIMED SPECIFICALLY AT THE collector of small and decorative furniture – larger than treen, but by no means architectural pieces. In fact, the sort of antique furniture you can put in the back of your car. It may be small but it is certainly not insignificant, for each piece reflects a period from our past as accurately as a painting or photograph. Each different timber and new design represents a development in our social history. For example, you will not find an Elizabeth I period tea caddy made of satinwood because we knew nothing of tea at that time, and satinwood had not yet been discovered. Take the dumb waiter, the davenport and the whatnot: each of these was designed to fulfil a specific need which had not existed before. It is the purpose, as well as the design and timber, that enables us to date a piece of furniture.

This is history; it is fun; and it makes the subject irresistible. Most of the small furniture brought in to the Antiques Roadshow dates from the second half of the 19th century. It was during this time that machine production revolutionized the furniture industry, enabling makers to include exotic veneers, luscious upholstery and fancy metal mounts cheaply and en masse.

Boxes and caskets are the most popular items, while small tables and chairs of every type come a close second and third. Perhaps the most common box is the travelling writing box, which opens to form a sloping lap desk. These are usually veneered with walnut or rosewood and

have a central brass plaque on the top for the owner's initials. Although military in appearance, most of these boxes were intended for the home civilian market. Since they are so common, they tend not to have great value, unless exceptional in every way; but this means they can be an ideal and inexpensive start for a collection.

Alternatively, small tables made after the 1780s can be modestly priced. Since they tended to follow the prevailing fashion, much can be learned from their design. Pairs of such tables are very rare and will fetch astronomically more than equivalent singles.

Much the same can be said for dining chairs – once again, singles are much cheaper than sets. I always recommend starting a collection with individual fine examples to create a harlequin set; each one is a conversation piece, while several will instantly add atmosphere to a dining room. A genuine, but not too grand, Chippendale period dining chair can be bought for less than £200, whereas a set of eight, all matching, can cost £10,000.

The subject of value always creates some confusion, especially when experts use different terms, such as "worth", "cost" or "insurance". The difference between these may be best explained by alluding to auctioneers who, to finance their operations, charge the vendor and the purchaser a commission. There is, therefore, a significant difference between what you get for something when you sell it – its "worth" – and what you pay for a piece when you buy it – its "cost". "Insurance" is a valuer's opinion of a future replacement cost.

WOODS & CONSTRUCTION

It is not always easy to identify the wood used for a piece of furniture because, although only a few types of timber were used, there has long been a tradition of making cheaper woods look like more expensive varieties.

Examine parts where the natural, unfinished wood is visible, but remember that parts not normally seen are often made from different woods from the rest of the piece. Sides of drawers, for instance, may be oak or pine, whatever timber is used elsewhere.

Strong, long-lasting native oak was used for the earliest English furniture: solidly made chests, chairs and tables. In the 1600s, oak began to be displaced by the more fashionable walnut. The most attractive pieces of wood – the burrs and curls – were taken from the weakest part of the tree and so were used mainly for veneers.

Mahogany came into wide use in the mid-1700s, when import taxes were reduced and after many walnut trees had been killed by frost.

FURNITURE WOODS

1 Oak: strong-grained wood that can vary from warm pale brown to almost black depending on the age and finish.

2 Beech: although plentiful and easy to work, it can warp.

3 Maple: less common pale wood, its "bird's eye" ringed grain was popular for veneers.

4 Walnut: faint grain with darker veining. Outgrowths produce popular burr veneers.

5 Rosewood: dark reddish-brown streaky wood used as a high-quality veneer.

6 Mahogany: rich copper-red wood which is usually stained rather darker.

FURNITURE PERIODS IN GREAT BRITAIN

STYLE	PERIOD	DATE	WOOD
GOTHIC	ELIZABETHAN	1558–1603	OAK PERIOD (UP TO 1670)
	JACOBEAN	1603–25	
BAROQUE	CAROLEAN	1625–49	
	CROMWELLIAN	1649–60	
	RESTORATION	1660–89	WALNUT PERIOD (1670–1735)
	WILLIAM & MARY	1689–94	
ROCOCO	WILLIAM III	1694–1702	
	QUEEN ANNE	1702–14	
	EARLY GEORGIAN	1714–60	MAHOGANY PERIOD (1735–1770)
NEO-CLASSICAL	LATE GEORGIAN	1760–1811	LATE MAHOGANY PERIOD (1770–)
REGENCY	REGENCY	1811–30	

WOOD GRAIN PATTERN

This depends on the part of the tree from which the plank is cut and the angle of the cut. **1** Quarter-sawn board. **2** Flat-sawn board. **3** Irregular figuring made by growth pattern of branches. **4** "Y" pattern at junction of main trunk and branches. **5** Veneers often cut from outgrowths.

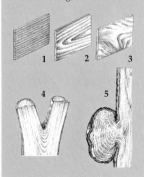

VENEERS & INLAYS

Chosen for their beautiful grain or figuring, veneers or thin sheets of wood were stuck to a plain wood carcass. Often different shapes and colours were assembled to form inlaid patterned bands (*above*) or floral (marquetry) or geometric (parquetry) designs.

The construction techniques and accessories used, as well as the type of wood, can help to date a piece of furniture and establish its authenticity.

Seats were made using plank construction, until, in the mid-1500s, joined construction was introduced. Early case furniture, such as the chest, was made using mortise and tenon joints held together with pegs and dowels; screws were first used in the early 1700s.

The frames, or carcasses, of case furniture were often quite crudely made of cheaper woods, such as pine, covered with a veneer. The backs of early pieces were not highly finished and may be composed of three or four boards secured with irregularly shaped nails; after c.1750 more care was taken and the backs were sometimes panelled.

Mouldings, styles of legs and feet, types of handles and methods of construction of drawers all give clues to the date of a piece of furniture. But it is wise to check that handles and feet have not been replaced with changing fashions and that table tops and legs belong together.

▷ **DATING WOOD SCREWS** *The handmade screw (1720–1830s) (left) has an uncentred drive slot, a filed top and uneven thread. The machine-made screw (mid-1800s) has a precisely centred drive slot, a lathe-finished top and milled thread.*

DOVETAIL JOINTS & MOULDINGS

Large handmade dovetail joints (**1**), secured with handmade nails, were usually present on the front edges of drawers until c.1700. In the early 1700s, the number of dovetails grew and they became more regular and equal in size (**2**).

Mouldings overhung the drawer (**3**) from 1725 to 1775, and until the 1760s they were sometimes part of the drawer front (**4**). After 1720, this style was used together with the cockbead.

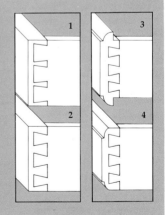

HANDLES

Shapes of handles were in keeping with the design of furniture, but many original handles have been replaced as a popular way of updating pieces. Early handles were of iron; later, steel was used, then brass, with the best quality ones gilded. From 1850 a wide variety of machine-made metal mounts appeared.

The dates given are only a guide as to when the handle type first appeared. **1** Iron drop handle, early 17th C. **2–4** Brass pendant handles, early 18th C. **5** Cast brass loop handle with engraved back plate, early 18th C. **6, 7** Cast brass loop handles, early 18th C. **8–11** Cast brass loop handles *c.*1750–1800; with pierced backplate (**8**); in French style with roses (**9**); decoratively cast with roses (**10**); swan neck (**11**). **12** Loop handle with stamped sheet-brass backplate, late 18th C. **13** Stamped brass knob, late 18th C. **14, 15** Cast drop handles, 1750–75; 1775–1800. **16** Regency star knob. **17–19** Victorian turned wooden knobs, often with ivory or mother-of-pearl inlay.

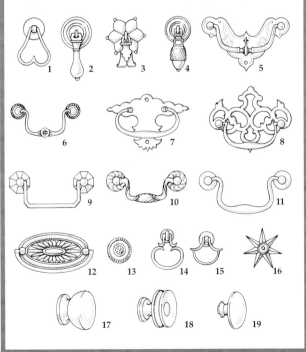

CHAIRS

In the Middle Ages, stools or benches
were the ubiquitous form of seating,
with chairs regarded as symbols of rank
and position; it was not until the 1500s that
chairs became more common.
The back stool – literally a stool with a
half back, which was far more portable than
earlier chairs – evolved in the early 1600s.
The great diversity now evident in
English chairs stems from the continental
ideas that reached the country after
the restoration of Charles II in 1660 and that
were spread by the Huguenot craftsmen
who flooded in some 25 years later.
By the 18th century, English chairs
had developed their own strong stylistic
trends, emphasized as the century
progressed by great designers such as
Chippendale, Sheraton and Hepplewhite.
With the introduction of machine-made
chairs during the 1800s, styles became more
eclectic and universal, until "reformers"
of the Arts and Crafts and Aesthetic
movements rebelled against mass
production and attempted to achieve
a purer style of hand-crafted chair.

DINING CHAIRS

By the early 18th century, English dining chairs had developed their own strong characteristics. They were made of walnut, had bold curved lines and a solid back splat and relied on the colour and pattern of the wood for decoration.

As the century progressed, the use of mahogany increased, and the simple lines of earlier chairs were embellished with carvings of shells and acanthus on crests, splats and knees.

The main designers were Chippendale, with his Rococo, Gothic and Chinese styles, and later Hepplewhite and Sheraton.

△ **WALNUT CHAIR**, *showing typical Queen Anne-style solid splat and turned back legs, combined with an outswept Chippendale-style back rail. 1710. Set of six £10,000*

▽ **CHIPPENDALE-STYLE CARVER**
A heavily restored mahogany chair with shell carving on the knee, which suggests that it may be Irish; one of a set of 10. 1750–60. **£800–£1,000**; *in good condition* **£3,500–£4,000**

18TH-CENTURY CHAIR STYLES

In the early 1700s, chairs were bold and curved, with little carving and solid splats. Carving increased over time, and by the 1750s splats were elaborately pierced and legs were straight or cabriole shaped. The fashionable styles ranged from Classical through Gothic and Rococo to chinoiserie.

1720–25

1750–55

◁ **MAHOGANY ARMCHAIR**
*This Chippendale-style armchair,
with delicately carved pierced,
interlaced splat and crested rail
in Gothic style are typical of mid-
18th century designs. 1760–65;
3ft high.* **£800–£1,200**

▽ **HEPPLEWHITE-STYLE CHAIR**
*made in mahogany, with a
Classical shield back in the
wheatear design. It is one of a
set of six which still have their
original covering of green hide.
Early 1800s.* The set **£3,500**

△ **LADDERBACK ARMCHAIR** *with
double-curved horizontal splats
and curved seat; one of a pair. 1770;
3ft 4in high.* The pair **£4,500**

1760–65   1765–80   1790–95

1765–70   1780–90

Chair styles were very varied in the 19th century. The Neo-classical styles of the late 1700s were still strong in the early years, but they were less delicate than those of Hepplewhite and Sheraton.

Regency dining chairs, with their curved top rails, sabre legs and reeded frames, were elegant. Carving was restrained, with motifs usually derived from Greek architecture and limited to the top rail and splat. In the late Regency and William IV periods, chairs had over-hanging top rails and straight legs. Then, over the next 20 years, a new form evolved in which the top rail merged with the upright supports to make a curved oval shape – the balloon back, at its height in 1850–70.

Later design was a hotch-potch of influences, among them Gothic, Elizabethan and Rococo, and those of "reformers" such as the Arts and Crafts Movement.

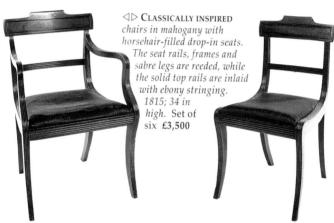

◁▷ **CLASSICALLY INSPIRED** *chairs in mahogany with horsehair-filled drop-in seats. The seat rails, frames and sabre legs are reeded, while the solid top rails are inlaid with ebony stringing. 1815; 34 in high.* Set of six **£3,500**

STYLES OF CHAIR BACK

Top rails were embellished with crests and shallow relief carving, while splats were usually simple or had pierced horizontal bars. Backs were also made in variations of trellis and X-shaped patterns.

OVERHANGING
TABLET RAIL

SOLID RAIL,
X-SHAPED SPLAT

SCROLLED CREST,
HORIZONTAL SPLAT

TABLET RAIL,
TRELLIS SPLAT

◁ **REGENCY DINING CHAIR** *A fine mahogany chair, one of a set comprising four side chairs and two carvers. It has an overhanging top rail, centre splats and turned, tapering legs. The seat is stuffed. 1835; 35in high.* The set **£2,500**

▷ **MAHOGANY ARMCHAIR** *that revives the Classical style popular 100 years earlier. The tapering legs with outswept feet and the cross bars below the X-framed splats are turned, and both top rail and seat rail are decorated with painted festoons. Late 1800s; 34in high.* **£500–£700**

◁▷ **BALLOON-BACK CHAIRS** *The deeply curved back and legs of the rosewood chair (left) are typical of the French Revival movement. 1860; 3ft high.* **£150** *Balloon-back chairs with deep upper rails (right, one of a pair) became highly popular in the late 19th C. 1875; 3ft high.* The pair **£300**

HALL & SIDE CHAIRS

From the reign of George II, chairs were placed along the entrance halls and corridors of large houses where people sat and chatted or visitors waited. These hall chairs, made originally of mahogany and later of oak, are distinguished by their solid unshaped seats. Side chairs, however, were more comfortable chairs that lined the walls of reception rooms for use when extra seating was needed.

The best hall chairs are those with architectural carving in the style of pilasters or formalized drapery. Some fine early 18th-century pieces with black or, in rarer cases, red lacquer decoration can also be found. Painted details, such as a family coat of arms or a crest, may help determine the original owner and location of a piece.

Sets of hall chairs are often now split into pairs or groups of four. Since demand is not great for these rather less comfortable chairs, superb examples of 18th-century craftsmanship can be found at affordable prices.

▽ **ROUT SEAT** *Such chairs were used to rest on during dances, known as routs. Their seats may be damaged from years of hard use, perhaps as a prop while the owner polished or tied his boots. 1760–80; 4ft high.* Set of six **£8,000**

TYPES OF HALL CHAIR

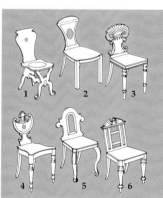

Chair design reflects the style of the period in which it was made: **1** George II curvilinear chair (1745–65). **2** Mahogany chair with tapered legs (1780–1800). **3** Carved shell-back chair with turned and reeded legs (1820–60). **4** Curved-back chair. (1840–80). **5** Georgian-style carved chair with cabriole legs (1870–1910). **6** Georgian-style square-framed chair (1880–1910).

△ **MID-VICTORIAN CHAIR** *The decorative details on this solid walnut chair include cabriole legs and a lozenge-shaped back with a central panel over a pair of "C" supports. 1865; 30in high.* **£150**

△ **MAHOGANY CHAIR** *Best described as being in French Baroque style, this Victorian side chair displays a typically 19th-century melange of earlier styles. 1860s; 30in high.* **£150**

△ **CHINESE EXPORT CHAIR** *This 18th-century-style* huang hua li *chair is typical of the furniture mass produced in China for the European market in this period. Late 19th century; 3ft 4in high.* **£400–£500**

△ **X-FRAME CHAIR** *A mahogany and walnut chair whose design derives from the "curule" chair of the Regency period, in turn adapted from the* sella curulis, *or stool, of ancient Rome. 1875–80; 35in high.* **£450**

△ **CAROLEAN CHAIR** *While not strictly a hall chair because of its padded seat, this type was often used as such. The barley-sugar twist supports and pierced frame were copied in the 1800s. 17th century; 4ft high.* **£450**

△ **WALNUT CHAIR** *The Baroque style of this highly ornate chair is intriguing; the curves of the upper back are in the form of new moons, but the carving on the lower part does not match. 1850; 3ft 10in high.* **£450**

COUNTRY CHAIRS

Made from locally available woods by provincial craftsmen, country furniture has its own style and charm. Country chairs were made in a variety of woods – including beech, elm, ash and yew – and their design varied from those traditional to the region to adaptations of the most fashionable styles.

The most popular country chairs are Windsor chairs. These were originally made of beech in the area of the Chiltern Hills. It was quite common for the chairs to be assembled from parts made by several local craftsmen and then taken to Windsor to be sold, hence the name. Nowadays Windsor chair is a generic term that is used to describe a style of chair.

Country chairs can often be bought very reasonably because they tend to be found as singles rather than in sets.

◁ **FINE OAK CHAIR**
Made in the late 17th century, this chair probably belonged to a wealthy farming family. The small pegs near the top are a good indication of age. They stick out because the wood has shrunk over the centuries. 1670–1700; 3ft 6in high.
£1,800

WINDSOR CHAIRS

Chair with Gothic-arch back and splats pierced like a church window (1750–90).

Chair with swept-back arms, cabriole legs and curved crinoline-type stretcher (1770–1830).

Simple, low-backed Windsor-style chair popular from the 1830s to the present.

▷ **ROCKING CHAIR** *The rather flat turning on this chair not only indicates that it was made by a provincial craftsman but also helps with the dating. Unusually, this chair is made of yew wood rather than the more common elm or beech. Although such chairs are attractive, they have proved quite difficult to sell. Late 19th century; 4ft high.* **£1,500**

◁ **TALL-BACKED BOX CHAIR** *The cheek-shaped panels on this chair were designed to protect the sitter from draughts. It was made using the frame and panel method. 1780–90; 4ft 5in high.* **£1,250**

▷ **COUNTRY ARMCHAIR** *The curious mixture of the highly fashionable vase-shaped splat, crest rail and pad feet together with the old-style turned supports and gap between the seat and back mark this oak armchair as a provincial interpretation of the latest London style. 1700–10; 3ft 7in high.* **£550**

OCCASIONAL CHAIRS

A great variety of chairs exists aside from upholstered and dining styles. Broadly termed occasional chairs, most of these pieces were intended for a specialized activity, such as reading, while others were kept simply as spare chairs.

One early form of occasional chair, which dates from at least medieval times, is the turned type, so called because it was made by turners rather than by joiners or carpenters.

In Georgian and Regency times an unusual form of library chair with an attached bookrest

was produced for use when reading or writing. Also popular at this time was the corner chair, with a leg at the front and back and two at the sides. Known in France as *fauteuils de bureau*, they were placed in the corner of a room for reading.

▷ **BEVAN CHAIR** *One of a pair of rare oak chairs designed by the architect Charles Bevan for the Leeds firm Marsh, Jones and Cribb. The chairs carried a patent and were made in a style favoured by the Arts and Crafts Movement. 1860s; 3ft 4in high.* **£5,000**

◁ **VICTORIAN REVIVAL CHAIR** *made of carved oak in what is intended to be Restoration style with a Spanish leather seat. The Victorian taste for reviving earlier furniture styles is much in evidence here. 1880; 20in wide.* **£300–£400**

△ **OAK SHIP'S CHAIRS** *Apart from the stretchers, the pair displays the Hepplewhite style and would once have been part of a larger set.*

Features that identify these as ship's chairs include brass number plates on the back; interchangeable cane or stuffed seats; and a bolthole through the centre of the stretchers which allowed them to be attached to the deck. 1900; 3ft high. The pair **£2,000**

◁ **WALNUT AND INLAID CHAIR** *Early 18th-century Dutch furniture, such as this, is attractive and often underrated. 1730; 17in wide.* **£200–£300**

▷ **WINGED ROCKING CHAIR** *with a side drawer. This is an uncommon example of a "lambing" chair since it is made of solid mahogany instead of oak, which is more usual. It may, therefore, have been made as a retirement present or a presentation piece. 1800; 3ft 4in high.* **£400–£600**

STUFFED CHAIRS

Fully upholstered chairs date from the late 17th century. The stuffing was mainly horsehair on a webbing base, with a wooden bar down the centre of the back and seat and a roll of horsehair along the front edge of the seat. Chairs became considerably more comfortable when, in 1828, coiled springs and then buttonback upholstery were introduced.

The materials for covering chairs changed with the new upholstery techniques. As well as leather, there was turkey work, a knotted pile fabric with patterns based on Turkish rugs.

Silks and velvet became fashionable in the 1700s; later, damask, patterned velvets and tapestry work were used. In the late 18th century brocaded satin and silks with striped or medallion patterns were common.

With the advent of mass-produced furniture in the 1800s, fabrics became cheaper.

◁ **ARMCHAIR WITH ROSEWOOD FRAME** *The high quality of this chair, with its scroll arms, baluster legs and serpentine-fronted seat, is indicated by the large amount of well-carved rosewood on show. 1865; 3ft high.* **£1,250**

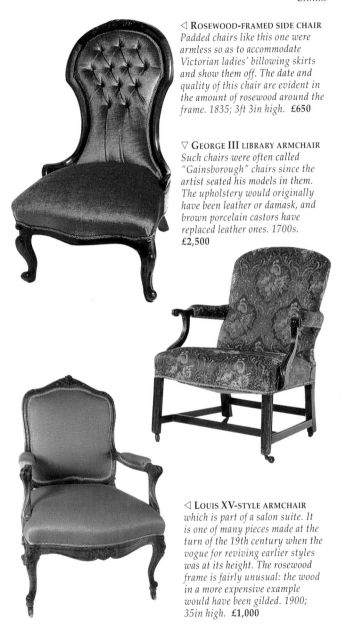

◁ **ROSEWOOD-FRAMED SIDE CHAIR**
*Padded chairs like this one were
armless so as to accommodate
Victorian ladies' billowing skirts
and show them off. The date and
quality of this chair are evident in
the amount of rosewood around the
frame. 1835; 3ft 3in high.* **£650**

▽ **GEORGE III LIBRARY ARMCHAIR**
*Such chairs were often called
"Gainsborough" chairs since the
artist seated his models in them.
The upholstery would originally
have been leather or damask, and
brown porcelain castors have
replaced leather ones. 1700s.*
£2,500

◁ **LOUIS XV-STYLE ARMCHAIR**
*which is part of a salon suite. It
is one of many pieces made at the
turn of the 19th century when the
vogue for reviving earlier styles
was at its height. The rosewood
frame is fairly unusual: the wood
in a more expensive example
would have been gilded. 1900;
35in high.* **£1,000**

TABLES

The types and sizes of tables have, over
the centuries, been governed to some
extent by the other uses to which the rooms
housing them have been put.
The first tables used in medieval great halls
were trestle tables – large planks of wood
supported on trestles – that would be
cleared away after the meal so that the hall
could be used for entertainments.
By Tudor times, the lord's family had
begun to dine in a separate room, which
resulted in the type of fixed table now
known as a refectory table. As the number
of smaller houses, and so demand,
increased from the mid-1600s, folding
tables became popular because they could
be moved out of the way when not in use.
Gradually, the range of tables made
for specific purposes grew to cater for an
increasingly sophisticated way of life, with
special tables for tea and cards among
them. The list was almost endless,
as was the skill and ingenuity displayed
in making the tables, in the woods used
and in their decoration with carving,
marquetry, ormolu and gilding.

SIDE TABLES

Intended to stand against the wall, side tables have been made since the 15th century. These tables, which were used as an additional surface at mealtimes or for holding ornaments, were among the first furniture to be made.

Yet they only became fashionable in the mid-18th century, when they were included in grand sets of furniture and were used both as writing tables and dressing tables.

A typical side table from this time can be identified by the overhang top supported on a rectangular frame; the single drawer; and turned, tapering or cabriole legs. It would usually

◁ **OAK SIDE TABLE**
Dating from the late 17th century, this joined table with bobbin-turned legs is in exceptionally fine condition. Opening the drawer reveals fine dovetails and cleat ends (narrow strips of wood for strengthening the top) which are all signs of quality craftsmanship. 1670; 30in wide. **£4,500**

THE EVOLUTION OF THE SIDE TABLE

The first side tables were box shaped and had outside stretchers. Early 18th-century designs were more ornate before returning to Classical styling later in the century.

1 Oak table with bobbin-turned legs (1690). **2** X-stretcher table with shaped apron (1700). **3** Early Georgian table with cabriole legs (1730). **4** George III square-legged table (1760).

have been made of mahogany, although oak, elm and beech were frequently used for less sophisticated pieces.

Two new types of side table developed during the 1700s. Console tables were attached to the wall and had only two front legs, although a mirror fixed behind them gave the appearance of four. Pier tables, as the name suggests, were designed to stand in a pier, the space between two windows.

▽ **MID-GEORGIAN TABLE** *Used as a lowboy, or dressing table, this piece is of exceptional quality. It has an attractive deeply shaped apron and cabriole legs ending in pad feet. 1755; 30in wide.* **£4,500**

▷ **CARVED OAK SIDE TABLE**
Although this provincial table was made in the late 1700s, its most noticeable feature – the extensive carving – dates from around 1900. In this instance, the carving is quite attractive. c.1770; 28in wide. **£800**

◁ **MAHOGANY SIDE TABLE** *from the mid-18th century with caddy-moulded overhang top. The cast brass swan-neck handle and escutcheon are typical of the period. 1750; 3ft wide.* **£2,000**

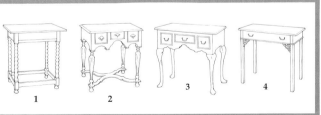

1 2 3 4

PEMBROKE & SOFA TABLES

Thomas Sheraton, the famous 18th-century designer, maintained that the Pembroke table was named after the Countess of Pembroke, since she was the first to order one.

These useful tables were generally rectangular or oval in shape with a single drawer in the centre and a hinged drop-leaf on each side. They were usually kept with the leaves folded down, but were opened when needed for meals, writing or drawing.

Although first made in the late 18th century, sofa tables only became popular in the Regency period. Designed to stand in front of a sofa, they were longer than Pembroke tables, usually had drawers on both sides and were often highly decorated.

▽ **SATINWOOD PEMBROKE TABLE**
This attractive table is beautifully painted with garlands of flowers along the frieze drawer and around the outside of the unusually shaped top. The turned and tapering legs, decorated with leaf patterns, can be used to date the table since they are sturdier than those made after 1800. 1785; 32in wide. **£25,000**

LOPER JOINTS

The narrow strips of wood that fold out to support the drop-leaves of a Pembroke table are known as lopers.

They were attached to the table using wooden hinged knuckle joints secured with a wood or steel pin.

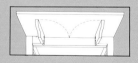

△▷ PAINTED PEMBROKE TABLE
In the 1780s, when it was made, this satinwood table would have been plain. The decoration of Neo-classical cherubs, flowers and festoons was added about 100 years later when painted furniture became fashionable. 1785; 4ft 2in wide. **£8,000**

△ SOFA TABLE
Decorated throughout with ebony stringing, this Regency rosewood sofa table rests on a tapering central pedestal and splayed legs. c.1810; 4ft 7in long (open) x 29in high. **£4,850**

OCCASIONAL TABLES

In the second half of the 18th century, society was stable and there was steady economic growth. These conditions produced a rapidly increasing group of middle-class and professional people requiring the trappings of an earlier and grander age – but accommodated in much smaller houses.

As a result, furniture was not kept in a set place but was moved around to suit the activities of the household. A circular tilt-top table, for example, would have been used as both a tea table at tea time and a supper table later in the evening. When not in use, it would have been pushed back against the wall, out of the way.

Likewise, drop-leaf tables were much in vogue because, with the flaps down, they took up little space, but provided a considerable surface area when opened up.

▷ MAHOGANY TEA TABLE
This tilt-top table started out quite plain. The ornate carving in imitation Georgian style was added to the top and legs much later. Mid-18th century; 31in wide. **£750**

◁ THIS GEORGIAN-STYLE TABLE'S *inlaid top and the painting on its curved imitation bamboo legs, which look back to Regency styles, are derived from Sheraton and Hepplewhite. c.1890.* **£1,200**

▽▷ **A fine Victorian table** *made of burr maple with gilt metal mounts and ebony and boxwood stringing. A band of stringing runs around the inlay on the legs, and the top has been delicately inlaid with ivory in the form of lily of the valley. c.1885; 27in high.* **£3,500**

◁ **French table à volets** *with four flaps (volet is French for shutter) which can be raised when needed. It is typical of a large number of tables made of ebonized wood, in cheap imitation of imported Chinese lacquer ware. The inlay is inserted into a panel of thuya wood from the Atlas Mountains. 1870; 3ft 3in wide x 3ft 3in high.* **£400–£600**

TRIPOD TABLES

The tripod table was at the height of its popularity in the Georgian period (1714–1811), when designers and craftsmen such as Chippendale were producing fine mahogany pieces.

Throughout this period, the basic design did not change, although the block at the base of the column disappeared after *c*.1750 and, from time to time,

different styles of leg were used.

The main variations were in the decoration. Some table tops had plain rounded edges, some were dished and others had a carved, scalloped edge known as "pie crust". A few had turned or fretwork galleries around the edge, and on those known as supper tables the top had recesses for plates or dishes.

△ CARVING *that is original stands proud of the leg (left); carving added later is cut into the previously smooth profile of the leg (right).*

△ MAHOGANY TEA TABLE
The legs of this table are carved to represent those of an 18th-century gentleman wearing buttoned breeches, silk stockings with elaborately tasselled garters and buckled shoes. Such pieces were known as Manxman tables – a reference to the three-legged emblem on the flag of the Isle of Man. 1750; 28in high. **£2,500**

ANATOMY OF A TRIPOD TABLE

This simple oak table has a plain top but also some sophisticated features. It was probably made by a country craftsman who was a turner, rather than a cabinet maker, since the column is finely detailed. The legs, top and birdcage mechanism – a complex feature that allows the table to rotate as well as tilt – are, however, quite crudely made. *c.*1740; 30in high. **£7,500**

△ *The brass catch locks the top in place when the table is in use.*

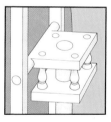

△ **BIRDCAGE MECHANISM**
The main column passes through a central hole in two blocks under the table. It is held in place (while being free to rotate) by the four small columns. To enable the table to tilt, two corners of the top block extend to form lugs, which connect to runners under the table top.

△ *The claw and ball foot (left) and the pad foot (centre and right) were used between 1740 and 1770.*

TEA TABLES

The ceremony and importance attached to making and drinking tea may be difficult to understand, but in the late 1600s, when tea drinking first became fashionable, tea was expensive and highly prized.

By 1727, when George II ascended the British throne, it had become customary to entertain friends to tea at home, and a variety of tables was made to cater for this. Among them were tilt-top tables, tables with fold-over tops, the ubiquitous little tripod table to hold individual cups, urn tables, kettle tables and highly decorative teapoys.

Popular during the 1800s, when more types of tea became available, teapoys were, in effect, large tea caddies on stands. They often contained as many as four small boxes holding different teas, which were then mixed in a central glass bowl.

◁ **A FRENCH-STYLE TEAPOY** *containing two boxes for different teas and a glass bowl for sugar. It is decorated with fine figured veneers, marquetry panels and ormolu mounts. 1870; 29in high.* **£2,000–£2,500**

▷ **CIRCULAR TEAPOY** *The galleried lid of this teapoy rises on an umbrella support to reveal two tea caddies and two glass bowls. 1830–37; 4ft high.* **£2,500**

▷ **MAHOGANY TEA TABLE**
This English tea table, with a scalloped top edge and apron and an under-tier, is typical of its period. Both the top and under-tier are inlaid with a floral design and decorative boxwood stringing, and there is stringing on the shaped legs and apron also. Early 1900s; 24in wide. **£350**

△ **REGENCY TEA TABLE** *A fold-over mahogany table with rosewood crossbanding and sabre legs ending in brass castors. The interior wood is a bright red and the inside well for storing table linen is still lined with the original blue paper. 1812–30; 34in wide.* **£2,000–£2,500**

CASTORS

1 Leather castor, mid-18th C. **2** Brass cup castor, late 18th C. **3** Brass square-toe castor, late 18th C. **4** Brass tapered cup castor, late 18th C. **5** Iron insert castor with earthenware wheel, 19th C. **6** Lion's-paw cast brass toe castor, early 19th C. **7** Cast brass toe castor, early 19th C.

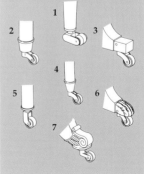

CARD TABLES

Boards for playing games such as backgammon and chequers have been in use since Tudor times. But it was only after the restoration of the English monarchy in 1660, under Charles II, that tables were made specially for games.

Most card tables were rectangular with a flap that opened up to reveal the lined playing surface. On early tables this lining tended to be velvet or needlework; baize became popular only in the early 1700s. When not in use, the flap was closed up and the table pushed against a wall.

In the Neo-classical period, semicircular card tables – the top opened to provide a circular playing area – became popular, and all tables were decorated with marquetry or crossbanding.

◁ **CONCERTINA CARD TABLE**
The fold-over top of this laburnum George II table rests on legs that extend using the concertina mechanism – a sign of quality. When open, the table is lined with green baize and has recesses for candles and money. 1730; 29in high x 35in wide. **£8,500**

Several mechanisms were designed to support the table flap. Which one was chosen for a particular table depended on when it was made and the quality of the piece.

Special tables were made for both games and cards. They usually had a well for playing backgammon and a reversible sliding top with a chess board marked on it.

Since card and games tables are decorative, compact in size and useful, they are highly sought after today.

◁ **VICTORIAN WALNUT CARD TABLE**
Decorated with highly figured walnut veneers, this fold-over card table has rather exuberant curvilinear supports. Although such flamboyance was popular in Victorian times, most card tables rested on a central pedestal. 1850; 31in high. **£3,000**

FOLDING MECHANISMS

Most card and games tables folded up so that they could stand against a wall when not in use. The quality and age of a piece determined the mechanism used. The simplest early tables had one or two hinged legs to support the flap (**1**). The more expensive concertina mechanism (**2**), introduced in the 1700s, had hinged sides that straightened as the back legs were pulled out. The hinge and swivel mechanism (**3**) was a sturdy 19th-century innovation.

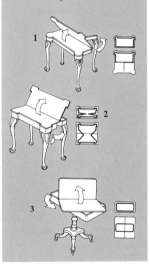

◁ **AMERICAN CARD TABLE** *When this mahogany table was made, many Europeans were migrating to America taking furniture styles with them. It is a mixture of the English Regency style with some Germanic and Rococo influence. The stencilled green baize is a rare feature. 1850s; 24in wide.* **£2,000**

WORK TABLES

Needlework accessories were, until the mid-1700s, kept in baskets or in the compartmented boxes used to hold lace. These were 12 to 14 inches long and were often covered in oyster veneer; it was a small step to mount such a box on a stand, so transforming it into a work table.

There were several variations on this basic design by the 1780s, and the prevailing Classical style is reflected in the work tables' straight, tapering legs and elegant proportions. By the 1830s designs were even more varied, and the Victorians borrowed from many periods and styles.

Tables were lined with fine, often brightly coloured, paper and had lids lined with silk; some have a deep silk bag.

△ **ROSEWOOD WORK TABLE** *Every middle-class family would have owned a work table such as this, which is typical of its period. It is, however, of better than average quality, with drop-leaves flanking the single drawer and a silk-lined bag. 1830s; 30in high.* **£2,500**

▷ **CONICAL WORK TABLE** *Although some of the marquetry is missing, this rosewood table with a walnut base is of good quality. Such tables are prone to woodworm and, if the base has been affected, can be found mounted on blocks of wood. Late 1800s; 3ft high.* **£350**

ANGLO-INDIAN WORK TABLE

This elaborately pierced and carved table is made of rosewood. It is a versatile piece that could be used as a sewing table – note the work basket underneath – and, less obviously, as a writing desk. Inside the drawer is a rising slope on which to rest a book.

This style was popular between the 1830s and 1860s. It would have been made by a local Indian craftsman to the order of an Englishman living in India at the time of the British Raj. 20in wide. **£1,500**

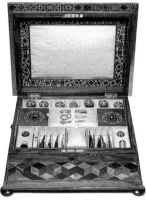

△ ROSEWOOD SEWING BOX *The type of inlay on this sewing box is known as parquetry – a form of marquetry based on a repeated, geometric pattern executed in woods of contrasting grain and colour. Here, the pattern on the exterior is carried through to the inside of the box and the fittings. c.1830; 14in wide.* **£1,200**

CHESTS &
CHESTS
OF DRAWERS

Typically constructed from native
and local woods, chests made of oak have
proved the most durable and, in
consequence, exist in the largest numbers
today. Collectors look for pieces that
display fine colouring and original carving,
and the survival of the original lock is an
added bonus. Chests of drawers were used
in virtually every room of the house from
the mid-17th century. As a result,
they form a large part of the antique
furniture around today, and good-quality
18th- or 19th-century examples can be
found relatively inexpensively.
Most desirable, however, are
well-proportioned, veneered pieces made
of fine quality timber in original condition.
Bombé and serpentine-shaped examples
command high prices, with smaller
chests also much sought after.

CHESTS

The earliest known type of furniture is the rectangular, top-opening coffer, or chest, and examples from ancient Egypt have been found. The earliest existing European chests, which were constructed rather than hollowed-out from logs, date from the 1200s. They are made of planks joined by nails; some of them have handles and are banded with iron for strength. By the 1500s, chests were of panelled construction, with mortise and tenon joints held by dowels.

Until the end of the 17th century, most fine chests were made of oak. In the 17th century drawers were added at the bottom of the chest, making access to stored items easier. Such hybrids were known as mule chests, and they remained popular throughout the 1700s.

Chests declined in popularity as cabinet-making techniques improved and chests of drawers became more widely available.

▷ **OAK TROUSSEAU BOX** *Such chests were used by brides for storing marriage clothes and linen. Foul-smelling candles were stored in a box inside the lid to deter moths. The carving is original and the existence of a key exceedingly rare. Early 17th century; 21in wide.* **£800–£1,200**

△ **PANELLED CHEST** *The precise and intricate, if fairly basic, chip carving displayed on this piece would have been made using a round punch and half-round chisel with the aid of a rule and compasses.*

Such designs using basic tools are typical of the time. The chest, which still has its original hinges, would probably have stood at the end of a bed for storing bed linen. 17th century; 4ft long. **£1,500**

△ **OAK BLANKET CHEST** *The original lock and hinges, and fine carving and colour, make this is a superb example of a panelled chest. With oak furniture, it can be difficult to differentiate between a genuine 17th-century piece and a 19th-century revival; carving was often added later. 1640; 3ft 6in long.* **£2,500**

△▷ **LARGE OAK CHEST** *with early Gothic carved front panels (right) and a superb lock plate with decorated borders. The panels are ecclesiastical in form and date from the 15th century, but the rest of the chest was made later. Oak was the standard timber for ecclesiastical fitments between the 9th and 15th centuries. 19th century; 4ft 7in long.* **£1,200**

CHESTS OF DRAWERS

From the mid-17th century, oak chests of drawers were widespread. Most examples seen today, however, date from the mid-18th century to the mid-19th century, with the majority made of mahogany.

When determining the age of a chest, a general overview can help establish its type. Bedroom furniture, for instance, is most often unadorned, while drawing room pieces are far more lavish and highly decorated.

Further information can be gleaned from the materials used, the construction, the drawer handles and the feet. Beware, however, when looking at handles, since they are easily

changed. This may be indicated by indentations on the drawer front and dissimilar woods.

In England after 1660, panel and frame construction was replaced by the European method of case construction. In this method, a carcass made of inexpensive wood is veneered with high-quality wood for a more sumptuous look.

A reliable guide to age is the slide mechanism on the drawers. Early pieces have drawers which pull straight out. From the late 17th century runners were used, until *c.*1710, after which drawer sides were made flat again. Side runners returned to vogue in the present century.

△ **LABURNUM CHEST** *with superb oyster veneering. While the feet are rather clumsy replacements, the handles are replicas of the originals. 1689–95; 3ft 4in wide.* **£12,000–£15,000**

CHANGING STYLES OF CHESTS OF DRAWERS

Early examples looked like chests but were, in fact, a set of drawers with cupboard doors on the front. By the 17th century, doors had been replaced by decorated drawer fronts.

The usual style, with drawers becoming deeper from top to bottom, was established by the early 18th century; later pieces were often simply larger, with more distinctive bracket feet.

Bow fronts were popular between about 1750 and 1775, with the deepest bows found on the finest pieces. After 1770, the serpentine top was added.

△ **EARLY OAK CHEST** *The joined construction and carved drawer fronts in this fine piece are of exceptional quality. The handles and feet are replacements, but the carving could date from the reign of James I (1603–25). Early 17th century; 3ft 3in high.* **£4,000**

STYLES OF FEET AND MOULDINGS

As well as the feet and the edge moulding along the top of a piece, grain pattern is a guide to age: before 1730, it runs down the moulding; after 1740 it runs lengthways.

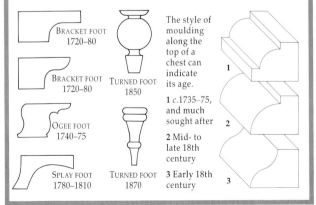

BRACKET FOOT
1720–80

BRACKET FOOT
1720–80

OGEE FOOT
1740–75

SPLAY FOOT
1780–1810

TURNED FOOT
1850

TURNED FOOT
1870

The style of moulding along the top of a chest can indicate its age.

1 *c.*1735–75, and much sought after

2 Mid- to late 18th century

3 Early 18th century

▷ **CHEST OF DRAWERS**
*A typical arrangement of
two short and three long
drawers is found below
the moulded overhanging
top of this simple chest. A
gentleman's clothes were
laid out and brushed on
the pull-out brushing
slide. The bracket feet are
original. 1775; 33in high.*
£2,500

▷ **GEORGE III SERPENTINE**
CHEST *There are four graduated
drawers and a brushing slide
below the eared top of this
mahogany chest. The canted
angles feature cluster columns.
On some such chests the top
drawer is fitted as a dressing
table. 1765; 33in high.*
£8,000–£12,000

◁ **AMERICAN KNEEHOLE**
CHEST *of a type seldom
produced outside Rhode
Island. This superb chest
in mahogany, ash and
tulipwood, with a typical
rounded block front and
stylized shell carving, is
attributed to the Townsend-
Goddard School in
Newport. Genuine
examples are extremely
rare and are valued at tens
of thousands of pounds.
1765–75; 34in high.*

▷ **TEAK MILITARY SECRETAIRE CHEST** *with drawer linings made of cedar. The top right-hand drawer front drops to form a writing surface, revealing several compartments for stationery and papers. Years of polishing have lent this piece an almost new look, but its construction dates it firmly to the second quarter of the 19th century. 1830; 3ft 3in high.* **£1,500**

CAMPAIGN CHESTS

First made in the late 18th century for officers on active service, the campaign, or military, chest came into vogue among the general public in the Regency and Victorian periods. Generally, it is these domestic campaign chests that have survived.

Most chests were made of teak or mahogany, with brass-bound corners, recessed handles and detachable feet for ease of transportation. As well as drawers, typical features included a mirror, wash basin and writing shelf.

◁ **WELLINGTON CHEST** *First made in the 19th century, such chests were named in the first Duke's honour. The left- and right-hand columns are hinged and lockable, and this burr walnut example would have been used to house coins, medals or specimens. 1845; 4ft high.* **£2,500**

OCCASIONAL FURNITURE

The term "occasional furniture" covers
a broad range of relatively small pieces.
Much of this furniture, which includes
fire screens and wine coolers, was designed
for an occasional, specific, purpose and
was moved around as required. Many
pieces were made as "one-offs", not as part
of a larger set. Other occasional pieces,
such as miniature cabinets, were simply
smaller versions of existing furniture.
Growing numbers of nouveau riche artisans
and professionals from the mid-18th
century onward created a demand for the
styles of a grander age and class – but
condensed for smaller houses.
Occasional furniture is, therefore, ideally
suited to the modern interior and is
in great demand today. When intending
to buy, personal taste will count for much;
but the finest quality pieces are those
that are in original condition and display
good craftsmanship, attractive detailing
and the use of fine timbers.

SMALL LIBRARY FURNITURE

U ntil the 1730s, books were owned mainly by the rich, and the bookcases built to hold them, often designed as part of the architecture of a big room, were also large. Then, in the late 1700s, it became fashionable to collect paintings so, to make more wall space, bookcases became smaller and revolving bookcases were introduced.

At the same time, many types of reading chair were made. These included the "horseman's" chair, common in Georgian times, on which the reader sat astride facing the back and rested his book on a stand attached to the top rail, and the upholstered armchair with a reading stand on one of the arms.

△ **PAINTED REVOLVING BOOKSTAND** *in an unusual mixture of West and East Indian satinwood. Such pieces, which were made from c.1890, copy those made 100 years earlier for drawing room use, but are smaller, and the painting is less sophisticated. c.1900; 4ft 10in high.* **£3,000**

▽ **REVOLVING BOOKSTAND**
An example of Edwardian Sheraton Revival style, decorated with stringing and crossbanding in a traditional manner. The three small drawers and cupboards make it a useful piece in a popular style. Early 1900s; 35in high. **£1,500**

◁ **MAHOGANY READING CHAIR** *with typical Regency splayed back legs and gadrooned front legs – features that became more marked as this type of chair continued to be made during the 1800s. The reading stand may have been replaced and the upholstery is not original. 1820–30; 3ft 4in high.* **£2,850**

▽ **BURR WALNUT WRITING SLOPE** *The cylindrical lid and inked-in walnut veneer of this writing slope are typically mid-Victorian. Original fittings include leather-covered tinder boxes with engraved metal lids, an inkwell, agate quill holder and gilt-metal paper knife. 1850s; 18in wide.* **£650**

◁ **WRITING SLOPE** *in polished mahogany. Although military in style, with brass-reinforced corners and flush-fitting handles, this substantial box was intended for civilian use. It still contains the original brass-lidded inkwells. 1850s; 21in wide.* **£800**

Like bookcases, writing tables and desks were also large until the advent of the *bonheur du jour* (a small desk made for ladies' boudoirs) and the davenport. In Victorian times, the easily portable writing slope or writing box was popular.

A davenport is a small desk with a sliding or pull-out writing slope, to accommodate the knees, and drawers that open to the side. The first such desk was, according to tradition, ordered by a Captain Davenport in the late 1700s, and early examples were in a plain, military style.

By the 1820s, davenports had become fashionable, and

▷ **FINE CYLINDER FALL DAVENPORT**
veneered in burr walnut and decorated with marquetry panels. On top is a stationery box, and the cylinder top conceals a rising slope for writing, pen trays and drawers. Shelves to hold sheet music replace the usual drawers. 1865. **£2,500**

styles in rosewood, mahogany and, later, burr walnut veneer became ever more ornate. In the mid-1800s, demand outran the supply of high-class pieces, and many inferior models appeared. Almost every type of davenport had been made by the 1890s, and the vogue for them waned.

STYLES OF DAVENPORT

Early davenports were box shaped and fairly plain but, as designs changed, features such as scroll legs became common. Sometimes drawers are hidden behind a door.

1 Scroll supports, flat top, 1865. **2** Scroll supports, piano-type top, 1865. **3** Turned supports, school desk type. 1840–85.

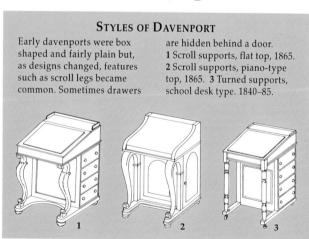

◁ **ROSEWOOD DAVENPORT** *with turned column supports in the Classical style and a bank of drawers for papers opening to the side. Around the top is a low brass gallery, and a small hinged drawer swings out to the side to hold the writer's pens and pencils. Early Victorian; 24in wide.* **£2,500**

▽ **BURR WALNUT DAVENPORT** *This ingeniously made piece has a counter-balanced rising top compartment for stationery and a writing surface which slides sideways to reveal a storage well. It is decorated throughout with split coloumn moulding, and the scrolling supports have fret-pierced panels. Mid-Victorian; 24in wide.* **£3,500**

Miniature Cabinets

The portability of miniature cabinets means that examples from all over the world can be found in salerooms, and since they are often extremely decorative, these cabinets are popular with collectors.

Most miniature cabinets made in Europe are contemporary copies of full-sized pieces, not, as is often thought, prototypes for larger pieces. They are sometimes called "apprentice's pieces", because it is believed that such cabinets were often made by trainee cabinet makers to show that they were sufficiently skilled to set up on their own.

Early cabinets were used for storing anything from spices to candles, lace, ribbons, needlework and silks.

△ **CHINESE BLACK AND GILT LACQUER CABINET** *made for the export market. The design was copied from an early 18th-century cabinet. 1810; 20in high.*
£400–£600

▷ **JAPANESE PARQUETRY CABINET,** *with painted lacquer doors; the unique style and the view of Mount Fuji on the inside of the lid confirm its origin. Such mass-produced pieces tend to be inferior in quality. Late 1800s; 17in high.* **£100–£130**

△ **APOTHECARY'S CABINET** *made in rosewood with brass inlays and fitted with glass jars and bottles and two drawers. Its solid style reflects the status of the physician. 1820s; 15in high.* **£400–£600**

MINIATURE SPICE CABINET

Such cabinets, which began to appear in England at the end of the 1600s, were used for storing expensive exotic spices. They could be wall mounted or free standing, like this example in yew with a neat arrangement of drawers, each with its original gilt drop handle. *c.*1690; 19in high. **£3,500–£4,000**

DUMB WAITERS & WHATNOTS

The first dumb waiters appeared in the 1740s. The basic form is a central column on a tripod base, with three circular trays of graduated size. The name "dumb waiter" is derived from its function as a receptacle for food from which guests could help themselves.

Until the 1770s, decoration followed that of tripod tables. After that, distinct variations began to emerge, with the widest variety of styles produced in the Victorian period. Trays are most often dished, with a lip around the edge, but the finest are those with galleries.

In the late 18th century the plain whatnot first appeared. Initially used as a receptacle for books and manuscripts, it soon became a general "holdall". Victorian variations on the form included the whatnot "canterbury" (music stand) and the writing desk, with bookrests and drawers. Decoration took the form of pierced galleries, carved and turned spindles, deeply shaped shelving, and veneers and marquetry.

By the 1890s the vogue was for plainer, 18th-century-style "Revival" pieces, and the heyday of the whatnot passed.

◁▷ GEORGIAN DUMB WAITERS *It is unusual to find dumb waiters in pairs: in this fine mahogany example, the columns between the three dished trays are turned in a matching design. The use of dumb waiters protected indiscreet guests against possible blackmail by unscrupulous staff. 1785; 4ft 4in high.*
The pair **£15,000**

△ **WALNUT WHATNOT** *A highly ornate design with drawers in the base. Many whatnots were made of walnut, as well as painted beech and cheaper timbers such as pine and fruitwood, with the most expensive pieces exhibiting the finest craftsmanship. 1850s; 5ft 6in high.* **£1,500**

△ **WALNUT VENEERED WHATNOT** *with decorative boxwood inlays and a mirror. This piece is typical of mid-Victorian furniture made in the East End of London. 1860; 4ft 4in high.* **£500–£800**

CHANGING STYLES

Despite their different purposes, dumb waiters and whatnots are often confused. The problem was compounded in the 1800s, when rectangular and square trays became popular on dumb waiters as well as on whatnots.

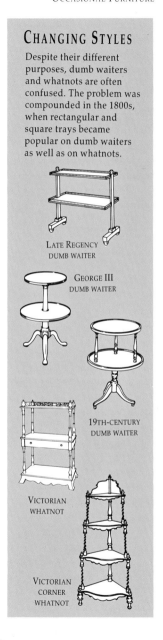

LATE REGENCY DUMB WAITER

GEORGE III DUMB WAITER

19TH-CENTURY DUMB WAITER

VICTORIAN WHATNOT

VICTORIAN CORNER WHATNOT

WINE COOLERS & CELLARETS

The terms "wine cooler" and "cellaret" refer to items with distinct uses. A cellaret is a box for storing bottles and may have a lead or baize lining; a wine cooler keeps wine chilled during a meal.

Wine coolers were first used in England and in fine houses were made of silver. Georgian designs were similar but used marble or granite. After c.1730 mahogany exteriors with lead-lined interiors, filled with ice, were common. They rested on a stand or sideboard pedestal.

Cellarets stood on integral feet or legs and could be round, square or hexagonal in shape. By the 1760s many had separate containers for bottles and ice. As bottles became taller in the 18th century, so cellaret design changed to accommodate them.

△ **MAHOGANY WINE COOLER** *with decorative brass banding made in the time of George III. The interior is lead lined and a tap on the base allows the water to be drawn off as the ice melts. 1770; 26in high.* **£4,850**

△ **TRAVELLING CELLARET,** *or decanter box. This piece is in excellent condition, complete with original bottles, glasses and stoppers made of fine Dutch glass. Fragile details such as these, if damaged, would seriously affect the overall value. 1800; 16in high.* **£2,000**

WINE COOLER SHAPES

The tapering box and curvilinear styles were popular between 1750 and 1780. After that, rectangular pieces found favour, with the sarcophagus common from the late Regency onward.

A REGENCY CELLARET

This 22-inch-high mahogany cellaret, made in 1830, is valued at £1,200. The design of such boxes had changed little since the 1780s, but the bulbous turned legs and the moulding on the top of the stand are Regency features. In the late 19th century many cellarets were converted into boxes for needlework.

Internal divisions create spaces to accommodate six bottles.

◁ **LARGE WINE COOLER** *made in the Hepplewhite period with bands of decorative brasswork and cast brass side handles. The base, with four square, tapered legs and brass castors, is original, as is the lead lining of the interior. 1770; 28in high.* **£4,500**

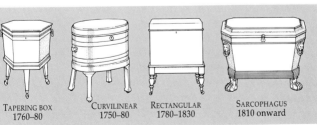

| TAPERING BOX 1760–80 | CURVILINEAR 1750–80 | RECTANGULAR 1780–1830 | SARCOPHAGUS 1810 onward |

FIRE SCREENS

Before the introduction of gas and electricity, fires were the major source of heat, consequently people sat close to them. It was not until the 18th century, however, that fire screens were widely used to shield the eyes from the glare when reading or doing needlework and to protect the face from the heat. This was particularly important, since wax was one of the main ingredients of cosmetics at the time.

Pole screens were generally made in pairs and consisted of a rectangular, shield-shaped or

▷ **ROSEWOOD POLE SCREEN** *This early Victorian piece, one of a pair, stands on a trefoil base and has a Berlin woolwork banner in a Rococo Revival shield-shaped frame. Although the original finial is missing, value is unaffected. 1835; 5ft high.* The pair **£1,500**

◁ **CHEVAL-TYPE SCREEN** *made in the 1920s by setting an 1845 sampler into an unadorned oak frame. Needlework panel screens date back to the early 1700s: a rectangular example attached to a wooden pole with a tripod base is illustrated in Chippendale's Director (1763). 1920; 28in high.* **£200–£300**

oval screen attached to a metal or wooden pole by a ring or screw, which allowed the height to be adjusted.

As well as pole screens for individual use, many 18th-century rooms had larger floor screens. These were known as "cheval" screens, from the French for horse, since they stood on four legs. A variation on the form was the fire screen desk, with a rectangular panel that pulled up at the rear. It was designed for use in the bedroom or smaller rooms of the house.

Fire screens were produced by leading cabinet makers of the period, such as Chippendale and Hepplewhite, while Ince and Mayhew sold mahogany-framed items with lacquer, silk or needlework decoration.

△ **GEORGE III PANEL SCREEN**
The English maker Thomas Chippendale supplied this mahogany fire screen. The canvas panels, depicting clematis and peonies, are of a later date. 1760–1830; 3ft 9in high. **£850**

FIRE SCREEN SHAPES

Adjustable pole screens from the mid-18th century typically display a simple elegance. In the Victorian period, shapes became more elaborate and opulent. With the increased use of gas for heat and light in the 19th century, pole screens became largely redundant. However, from the late 1800s onward larger cheval screens were favoured. The early 1900s saw the revival of popular Regency styles (see example from 1820).

1775   1780   1855

1820   1860

SMALL PINE FURNITURE

Pine, also known as deal, is a pale yellow to reddish softwood with a straight grain, which has long been used by European furniture makers. In areas where it was readily available, such as Scotland, Austria and Scandinavia, pine furniture was common; elsewhere, much of the pine was imported from the Baltic and later in the 1800s from North America.

City craftsmen employed pine mainly for drawer linings, backboards and carcasses that were later veneered in superior woods such as walnut. Country makers produced a wide variety

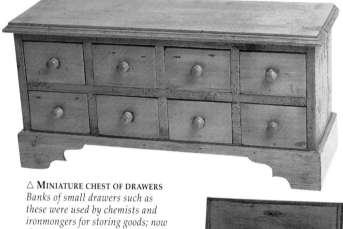

△ **MINIATURE CHEST OF DRAWERS**
Banks of small drawers such as these were used by chemists and ironmongers for storing goods; now they are bought mainly for use in the kitchen. When it was made, this piece was probably scumbled to resemble a more expensive wood. 1800; 30in wide. **£250**

◁△ **AUSTRIAN DEED OR BIBLE BOX**
with the original hand-forged iron strap hinges and fitted with an interior box for holding candles. The painted decoration, too, is original. 1840; 32in wide. **£300–£500**

of well-made pine furniture and other small domestic pieces.

Much country furniture was made by local carpenters and joiners using early construction methods, but in the 1800s, pine furniture was made both by hand and by machine in country styles. Handmade pieces are more expensive: they look less regular, the planks are generally wider, and the wood often has better colour and grain.

Although continental pine furniture and boxes were often painted, either in flat colours or with floral motifs, in Britain it was more usual for the wood to be scumbled. In this process, a piece of furniture was varnished and, while the varnish was still wet, the surface was combed or brushed into grain patterns similar to those of more desirable woods, such as mahogany and walnut.

▷ **STRIPPED BOW-FRONTED COMMODE,** *or chamber pot holder, with turned legs in the style popular at the time of William IV. A simulated mahogany grain pattern would almost certainly have been applied to this piece by a specialist workshop when it was made, but this finish has been removed. 1840; 29in high.* **£350–£400**

◁ **SUSSEX PANTRY TABLE** *The peg-jointed construction, short splayed legs and simple carving on the drawer front give this small piece a sturdy, unsophisticated air – a quality the Arts and Crafts Movement consciously strove to capture in their furniture later in the century. 1860s; 18in high.* **£400–£450**

CHILDREN'S FURNITURE

Apart from cradles and high chairs, children's furniture is really just a smaller model of adult furniture. It is generally of good quality since most of what survives today was commissioned by wealthy parents. The richer the family, the more faithful and elaborate the piece.

▽ **MAHOGANY CRADLE** *The design of this fine quality cradle is copied from oak cradles made in the late 1600s and early 1700s. The true date of the piece is, however, given away by the wood used and by the stylized sunflower on the back, a motif favoured in late Victorian times. 1885; 3ft 2in long.* **£500**

STYLES OF CRADLE

The best early cradles were made of oak; later examples were constructed of mahogany, cane and even wrought iron. Cradle styles developed from the simple carved box on rockers to the more sophisticated boat shape on a swing frame which kept the baby off the ground.

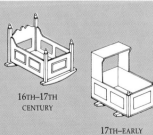

16TH–17TH
CENTURY

17TH–EARLY
18TH CENTURY

Even famous makers, such as Thomas Chippendale, made furniture for the children of their most important clients.

Most children's furniture was a small-scale version of the adult piece. It should not be confused with dolls' furniture or traveller's samples, which tend to be too small for use.

Chairs are the most common pieces of child's furniture found today. They were first recorded in Elizabethan times, when they were similar to those of adults, but had longer legs.

◁ **OAK HIGH CHAIR** *Made during the reign of Charles II, this piece would originally have had finials on its top. It is very similar to the type of chair the child's parents would have used, albeit with longer legs. It has a carved back panel, scrolled arms and turned legs joined by square stretchers. 1660–85; 32in high.* **£4,000**

▽ **BENTWOOD ARMCHAIR** *This type of chair, invented by the Austrian Michael Thonet, derives its name from the way the frame was bent using steam. Popular since the 1830s, millions were made. This child's version still has its maker's label. 1890; 27in high.* **£125–£175**

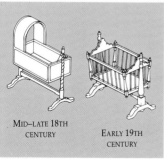

MID–LATE 18TH CENTURY

EARLY 19TH CENTURY

In the 18th century, children's chairs imitated the sophisticated curvilinear lines of the adult Queen Anne pieces. As with earlier children's chairs, the legs were extra long. During this century a new type of miniature chair developed. It stood on a movable platform which could double as a child's table. This design was the forerunner of the high chair and could, by 1800, be attached by means of a coach bolt to the edge of a table.

Cane was first imported for use in chair making in the time of Charles II. It was split and woven to produce seats and chair backs not only for adult chairs but also for the miniature

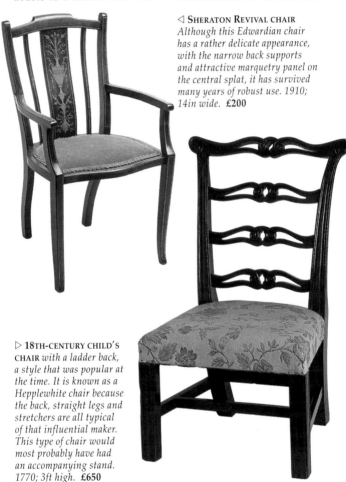

◁ **SHERATON REVIVAL CHAIR**
Although this Edwardian chair has a rather delicate appearance, with the narrow back supports and attractive marquetry panel on the central splat, it has survived many years of robust use. 1910; 14in wide. **£200**

▷ **18TH-CENTURY CHILD'S CHAIR** *with a ladder back, a style that was popular at the time. It is known as a Hepplewhite chair because the back, straight legs and stretchers are all typical of that influential maker. This type of chair would most probably have had an accompanying stand. 1770; 3ft high.* **£650**

versions used by children. These diminutive models had the added charm of baluster- or bobbin-pattern turned uprights that were out of proportion to the rest of the chair.

As time progressed children's furniture continued to be made in a huge variety of styles reflecting the prevailing fashion.

▷ **CHILD'S WINDSOR CHAIR**
The turned leg and arm supports and the pierced splat on this fine hoopback chair are exact replicas of those found on the full-size chairs. It was constructed using two woods: yew and beech. 1850; 3ft 4in high. **£650**

PAPIER MÂCHÉ CHAIR

Made from layers of paper pulp moulded and pressed into shape, papier mâché originated in the East. In Victorian times, it became very fashionable to make small furniture, such as this chair, by moulding papier mâché on a metal or wooden frame.

The original seat of this early Victorian chair would have been made of cane.

When the present seat was put on, in the early 1900s, it was painted to match the attractive Japanese-style decoration on the back. *c.*1840; 17in high. **£185**

COLLECTOR'S CHECKLIST

PROBABLY THE MOST ENJOYABLE aspect of collecting antique furniture is that every piece is a tangible item of history – part of the society of an earlier period.

You should not be afraid of antique furniture. Just as a house needs to be lived in, so furniture needs to be used. A family dining table made in 1760, for instance, should still be enjoyed. With care and normal use, it has lasted until today, and with the same treatment it should continue to offer good service for another 200 years or so.

Encourage children to use, and respect, antique furniture, for in this way they will grow to enjoy our heritage.

There is no real mystique to antique furniture: understanding it is merely a logical process, but with experience and appreciation of manufacturing techniques and design styles comes deeper knowledge.

When you look at a piece, mentally check that its use, the material it is made from, its shape and decoration had all been "invented" at the time the piece was supposed to have been made.

For example, there will be no Elizabethan satinwood teapoys with Classical decoration. First, tea was not known in the West; second, satinwood was not used for furniture; and, third, cabinet makers knew little of Classical decoration.

Antique furniture in perfect condition is usually prohibitively expensive, but many collectors buy pieces in need of restoration. However, it is important to check that a piece is worth restoring. It should be missing few elements (brass inlay or ormolu mounts can be extremely expensive to replace) and to merit restoration the wood should be of fine quality and not too badly warped, since the work of professional cabinet makers does not come cheap.

The method of construction will help to establish the date at which furniture was made. From the end of the 15th century until well into the 17th, most joints on chairs and other furniture were of the mortise and tenon type. Until c.1700, two large dovetail joints were used where the end grain of wood was joined to the side grain (as with drawer corners); after that date, dovetails became more numerous and more precise.

Styles of handles, locks, castors, screws and hinges, and the materials from which they were made, can all be dated to a greater or lesser extent, and all help to establish authenticity.

The style of the feet and legs on a piece of furniture can be another good indication of period. Even styles that were reproduced at a later date have subtle differences which allow them to be distinguished from the original. For instance, 18th-century cabriole legs were usually more finely carved than those on later reproductions, which took a more exaggerated form.

"Earpieces" at the top of cabriole legs were always made separately and glued on. Replacements can be spotted by comparing the colour and carving with the rest of the leg.

TIPS FOR BUYERS

1 Look carefully at the colour of the wood. On an exposed surface it will be fresh and dry. In hidden areas it will be darker, but still dry. The build-up of grease and wax, naturally leading to a mellow colour, is termed patina and is almost impossible to fake.

Patina does not build up evenly; in places such as the top rail of a dining chair, or the overhang of a fold-over table, where hands have held or lifted it, oils from the skin will have helped to created a good patina, slightly darkening the wood. It takes many years for a good patina to develop.

2 Chests of drawers have often had several sets of handles. The way to detect this is to check inside the drawer fronts for holes which may have been filled and disguised. A layer of dirt and grease will have accumulated around handles that have been on a piece for a long time, and they may have marked the front of the drawer where they have knocked against it.

3 Deep 18th-century chests of drawers have often been made narrower. Take out a drawer and check that the grooves for the drawer runners stop short of the backboard and that the dovetails on drawers are all of the same quality.

4 Victorian bow-fronted chests vary little from those of the 18th century in basic structure, but details such as a heavy overhanging top and bulky feet can be a guide. Check closely for disguises in both places.

5 Table tops are often married to legs that do not belong to them; for instance, small tripod tables are sometimes made up with legs taken from a fire screen. Where the pedestal meets the underside of a tilt-top table, the marks on both parts should correspond.

6 The underside of the top of a gate-leg table should show the marks caused by the legs being pulled out and where the top has rested.

7 Table edges should show the signs of many years use; too perfect an edge suggests that the top may have been cut down or heavily restored.

8 Check that areas of wear on the top rails and stretchers of chairs are genuine and that they have not been artificially "distressed". Wear should show mainly on the front stretcher, where feet have been placed.

9 The feet on furniture can be a useful indicator of period, although there may be pitfalls, since, like handles, they were sometimes altered to reflect the prevailing fashion or to replace worn original feet. Replacement feet do not necessarily detract from a piece unless they are out of style.

10 Original carving always stands proud of the outline of a piece; it is never recessed. In the same way, 18th-century beading was carved from wood left on a piece of furniture for that purpose, so the grain pattern will be true; by contrast, Victorian beading was carved separately and then glued in place.

POTTERY &
PORCELAIN

POTTERY & PORCELAIN

THE COLLECTOR OF CERAMICS, LIKE ALMOST ANY collector, has to set limits, often arbitrary, on what to buy. With several thousands of years of production worldwide, the range of objects from which to choose is greater than in any other field. Identifying what one is holding in an antiques market may not be easy: on a modern piece most of what one needs to know may be stamped on the back. On an older piece one may only be sure that what one is holding is a plate. For that reason, this book has been arranged by class of object.

Most ceramics – that is, wares made of clay and fired – were for practical use. Some were apparently made as such but, as in China during the Song Dynasty (960–1279), were actually for burial with the dead for use in the afterlife. Even vases, which seem to serve no function but display, may have served as urns for ashes in Roman times or as prizes at the Greek games. Some of these ancient wares, surprisingly perhaps, are not beyond the pocket of the ordinary collector; for instance, a Roman terracotta lamp, 2,000 years old, may cost under £100. The problem is that the cheaper forms run out quickly and then there is a sudden jump in price to thousands of pounds.

But from only the last 200 years of ceramic history in Europe, the collector has an almost limitless choice of form, material, country, factory or artist at prices from a few pence to over £1,000,000. Objects are gradually shuffled along the conveyor belt of time, starting as a cheap teacup at one end and ending as the Holy Grail at the other. With the change in attention goes a rise in price.

It is no coincidence that this little book is largely given over to tablewares – tea, coffee and dinner services. More of these exist than anything else and more are 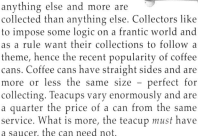 collected than anything else. Collectors like to impose some logic on a frantic world and as a rule want their collections to follow a theme, hence the recent popularity of coffee cans. Coffee cans have straight sides and are more or less the same size – perfect for collecting. Teacups vary enormously and are a quarter the price of a can from the same service. What is more, the teacup *must* have a saucer, the can need not.

Tea has held a special place in English society for 300 years and the vast range of tea wares reflects this. Tea wares and mugs are suitable vehicles to record the British affection both for its monarchy and for other more transitory events, and such commemorative wares have survived in large numbers.

The market at present has a distinct dislike of damage: the minutest chip or hairline crack will put off most buyers, and the price of a damaged item will be, perhaps, a tenth of that of a perfect piece. But for the true collector, who would rather have something damaged than not at all, trading up when a good example comes along, times have never been better. It must be said, however, that the damaged piece will never have the investment potential of a perfect one. One should, however, be buying for pleasure, not for investment.

The History of Ceramics

Although the history of ceramics appears complex, there are several broad patterns that run through it.

During prehistoric times, it was discovered that clay could be fixed in a shape by drying it in the sun and, presumably by accident, that fire could create a more lasting effect. At that time, the potter's art was born. Over the centuries, techniques were developed for shaping clay and for refining the clay body, which developed from the basic, porous earthenware to the more robust stoneware that was watertight when fired.

The discovery and development of glaze was another major advance. Not only did a clear glaze seal and enhance the colour of the underlying body, but it could itself be coloured by adding a metallic oxide, resulting in an almost infinite variety of glaze colours and textures.

Developments occurred in many places at different times due to local evolution, conquest or trade. No culture was more prolific than that of China, where the advent of the potter's wheel in the 2nd millennium BC revolutionized pottery and led to the refinement of clays necessary for throwing.

Many centuries later, during the Tang Dynasty (618–907),

△ *Imitation-Meissen porcelain plate.*

stoneware was refined into the white translucent body known as porcelain or china. It was to take a further thousand years and hundreds of experiments in soft-paste, or artificial, porcelain before Europeans were able to produce their own hard-paste, or true, body.

It was the growing awareness of Chinese porcelain in the 1300s to 1600s that gave impetus to porcelain-inspired alternative traditions both in Renaissance Europe and in Islamic lands. The use of tin glaze – clear lead glaze with added tin ashes – turned buff-coloured pottery white. This allowed it to be painted and gave rise to some of the most popular European pottery.

△ *Salt-glazed stoneware cup.*

△ *Early tin-glazed earthenware (maiolica) wet-drug jars.*

This tin-glazed earthenware flourished in the 1300s and 1400s in Spain, where it was known as Hispano-Moresque, and in Italy, where it was called maiolica. Over time, migrants spread the tradition northward. As production was started in different countries the name of the wares evolved: delftware in England; Delft in the Low Countries; faience in France; and *fayencen* in Germany and Scandinavia.

Once trade with the Far East was under way, the arrival of Chinese and Japanese blue and white porcelain had far-reaching effects on the European earthenware and stoneware industries. It inspired the search for hard-paste porcelain and the refining of more traditional bodies, and led to much artistic imitation of both blue and white wares and colourful Japanese designs.

Around the same time, the formula for true porcelain was discovered and exploited at the Meissen factory near Dresden. For 40 years, only Meissen, and the Du Paquier factory in Vienna, produced hard-paste porcelain. But by the 1750s, Meissen's shapes and decoration were widely imitated in Europe.

It was an earthenware potter, Josiah Wedgwood, who brought the Industrial Revolution to ceramics when he set up his Staffordshire factory in 1759. He improved clay bodies and firing techniques; set up production lines; and used modern marketing techniques.

In the late 18th century, three developments – transfer printing; slip casting; and the creation of the hybrid "bone china" – gave English potters an edge. Allied to the political decline of China in the 1790s, they gave the European industry, especially in England, trading supremacy.

△ *Lead-glazed slipware tyg, or cup.*

BODIES & GLAZES

All pottery and porcelain is made from clay which has been hardened by fire. In most instances, the clay has also been refined to create a "body", or paste, with particular qualities of colour and plasticity.

Learning to recognize the material used is the first stage in identifying and dating ceramics; hence the importance of examining the bottom, or foot, of an object where the unglazed clay can be seen.

There are two basic bodies: porous earthenware, which is fired to 900°F–1,500°F; and non-porous stoneware and porcelain, fired to c.2,400°F. Porcelain, also called china, can be distinguished from stoneware by its translucency and whiteness. It is divided into two types, soft-paste, or artificial, porcelain and hard-paste, or true, porcelain, which originated in China.

The term "bone china" refers to a special type of soft-paste

△ *A Wedgwood pot being thrown.*

porcelain to which bone ash has been added. Developed in the late 1700s in Staffordshire, it had been adopted by most English factories by the early 1800s.

The next most important constituent of a piece is the glaze. By applying a glaze, a potter modifies or covers the body. A clear lead glaze, for instance, will convert the buff colour of Staffordshire slipware to a honey tone. An opaque tin glaze covers the body in a white "skin" which can then be painted. Being able to recognize types of glaze is important in identifying a ceramic piece.

The decoration of a piece follows the body and glaze in importance. Lead glaze lends itself to in-glaze colour stains, such as those used on the

△ *Transfer printing Spode's Italian pattern.*

△ *Gilding: the final stage of ornamentation.*

Staffordshire vegetable moulded wares of the 1700s. Monochrome glazes, including browns, reds, blues and spectacular yellows, were perfected by the Chinese. Porcelain glazes are often transparent and colourless to show off the whiteness of the body and give it a sparkle.

In the 1300s, the Chinese found that cobalt blue painted on a piece before it was glazed matured to a strong blue colour when fired. Such metallic oxides, applied and fired under the glaze, are known as underglaze pigments. This discovery was widely copied in both earthenwares and porcelains, all of which are known as blue and white or underglaze blue wares.

Other decoration could be painted or enamelled on top of the glaze. Ceramics may be hand painted or decorated with mass-produced transfer prints; some are even gilded.

Valuable clues for identifying pottery or porcelain can also be derived from the construction method and from the presence of moulded decoration. Neolithic pots were made by building up coils of clay or fixing slabs together. Later came the potter's wheel and throwing followed, later still, by slip casting. The inside of a piece is more likely to divulge the construction method than the finely finished outside.

Moulded decoration can be cut out, impressed, scored or stuck on. Classical friezes were applied to Wedgwood pieces whereas imitations are often part of an all-in-one slip mould.

△ *Cleaning up applied motifs.*

Tea &
Coffee Wares

Since the mid-17th century, when tea
arrived in the West from China and began
to be drunk in coffee houses and later
at home, tea and coffee wares made in
a wide variety of styles have been among
the most popular ceramics. For collectors,
the appeal of tea and coffee wares lies
in their almost infinite variety: of
form, decoration, material, country
of origin and style. What is more, prices
range from a few pounds to thousands.
The growing trend toward collecting
one particular shape – teapots or coffee
cans for example – means that most
services are broken up and the pieces sold
individually. The wide range of damaged
pieces is an invaluable storehouse
for the tyro collector.
A cracked tea bowl, for instance, bought
for just a nominal amount, can prove
the perfect learning tool. Buying damaged
and upgrading is an old-established
and sensible procedure.

JUGS

It is little wonder that jugs are some of the most common antique ceramics, for they were among the most used domestic items. Milk was measured from the churn into a jug on the doorstep; water was collected from the well or pump in a bucket and ladled out with a jug; and even in the early 1900s, beer and cider were usually fetched from the pub in a jug.

In Britain, early jugs were mainly earthenware; later, stoneware and parian, both of which can be easily moulded, predominated. Jugs are of particular interest to collectors, since they often bear dates, makers' and Registration of Design marks.

△ **STONEWARE JUG** *with stamped and incised decoration typical of the Westerwald region of Germany; the silver mount is a 19th-century addition. c.1690.* **£3,000–£5,000**

△ **ENGLISH CREAMWARE JUG,** *thought to have been made in Newcastle or Sunderland, since it carries the inscription "John & Ann Fletcher Hexham", who were probably a local couple. It would have been used for milk or ale. 1792; 9in high.* **£750–£1,000**

◁ **ENGLISH JUG** *with a traditional fox-hunting scene moulded on the stoneware body, and the neck and handle covered in a vibrant blue enamel. It was made in Staffordshire by Turners, but many other factories produced similar wares. Early 1800s; 9in high.* **£70–£100**

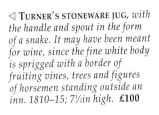

▷ **TURNER'S STONEWARE JUG,** *with the handle and spout in the form of a snake. It may have been meant for wine, since the fine white body is sprigged with a border of fruiting vines, trees and figures of horsemen standing outside an inn. 1810–15; 7½in high.* **£100**

▷ **BONE-CHINA JUG,** *moulded with daisies, which was used for lemonade: the strainer at the base of the spout would have trapped the pips. Jugs of this type were mass produced in Staffordshire; this one was made by Graingers in Worcester. 1840; 8in high.* **£60–£90**

◁ **MOCHAWARE JUG** *This large jug, which was used to carry beer from the cellar of an inn to the bar, has a second handle beneath the spout. The words read: "The population of Kent in the year 1841 was 54861". The jug would be worth more if it were not slightly damaged. 9½in high.* **£200–£500**

▷ **SCOTTISH STONEWARE JUG,** *which is unusual in that it is decorated with pictures of giraffes in lustre. It was made in Glasgow as a wedding gift and is owned by a direct descendant of the marriage partners. 1875; 8in high.* **£75–£100**

MUGS

The term mug describes a drinking cup with a single handle and a rim without a lip. It is smaller than a tankard and generally does not have a lid.

Mugs were first made in England in the 16th century and soon took the place of beakers. Eventually, as well as earthenware and stoneware examples for everyday use, fine china mugs, painted with scenes and flowers and often also gilded, were produced by all the major factories.

△ **DERBY MUG** *of characteristic shape, with ribs at the top and bottom and a fine painting of birds in fresh colours on a very white body. Typical spin marks from the wheel can be seen under the base. Its present owner bought it many years ago for £3.10s, which was then his weekly wage; it has proved a good investment. c.1757; 6in high.* **£1,750**

△ **WORCESTER MUG** *painted in two shades of cobalt blue with a rare design (now known as "The Gardener") showing a Chinese man, a vase of flowers on a table and a kneeling boy at the side. 1765–70; 5in high.* **£700–1,200**

▷ **FAMILLE-ROSE MUG** *Export wares from China were popular in 18th-century Europe. This attractive mug has intertwined handles and delicate floral decoration in the soft coloration typical of* famille-rose *pieces. c.1785; 8in high.* **£500**

◁ **PEARLWARE MUG**, *probably from a Welsh factory, with a transfer-printed and hand-enamelled steeplechasing design. The name "pearlware" derives from the bluish glaze. The piece is also heavily stained where liquids have penetrated the crazed glaze. 1830s; 3½in high.* **£25–£35**

▷ **ROCKINGHAM MUG** *made in the pottery set up c.1745 by the Earl of Rockingham on his Yorkshire estate. In 1826–47 it also made porcelain pieces, such as this mug depicting the London to York mailcoach, which features Rococo gilded decoration typical of the factory. c.1835; 5in high.* **£1,000**

JOKE LOVING CUP

Frog cups and mugs, such as this ironstone one, have been surprising unwary drinkers since the 1600s. A name and date appear on the mug, so it may have been a christening gift. 1850; 5½in high. **£300**

▷ **CIDER MUG** *in Sunderland lustre. Despite the name, such wares were also made in Liverpool, Bristol and Staffordshire. Purple lustre laid over the glaze was sprayed with oil blown through a muslin-covered tube. In the kiln, the oil expanded and formed bubbles which burst, producing characteristic irregular blotches. c.1860; 3½in high.* **£120**

COMMEMORATIVE JUGS & MUGS

Events of historic importance, whether they be the death or coronation of a monarch, the first ascent in a balloon or landing of a flying boat, have long been marked by the production of ceramic mementos.

Delftware items were produced in the 17th century to celebrate the restoration of Charles II; Queen Anne was honoured in the same way; and most British rulers since have been similarly commemorated.

In the early 1800s, potters made slip-cast jugs relating to the Napoleonic Wars. Politics and sport, too, were exciting subjects, and the deeds of famous men, from William Gladstone and Winston Churchill to pugilists, are marked on jugs and mugs.

◁▷ **STAFFORDSHIRE JUG**

A rare piece that commemorates the death of the much disliked King George IV. The portrait is very flattering: he weighed 20 stone and is said to have had a spherical body. Where the glaze is thin, the pottery is discoloured, which reduces the jug's value. 1830; 5in high. **£140**

△ *The base of the jug bears the initials W B for William Brownfield's factory and the registration code for 1863.*

△ **WHITE STONEWARE JUG,** *smear glazed and moulded with the coats of arms of England, Scotland, Ireland and Wales, and insignia such as the Prince of Wales's feathers and* Victoria's cypher. *It was made in Staffordshire to mark the marriage of Albert Edward, later Edward VII, to Princess Alexandra of Denmark in 1863. 6½in high.* **£80–£120**

DOULTON JUGS

As these stoneware jugs from Doulton's Lambeth factory show, political and sporting figures, such as Disraeli (*left*) and the cricketer W.G. Grace (*below*), were popular subjects for commemorative wares.

△▷ *Jug with moulded and incised decoration, honouring Benjamin Disraeli (above), 1881; 8in high.* **£100–£150**. *Printed cricketers jug (right), 1890s; 7½in high.* **£200–£300**

△ **VICTORIAN DIAMOND JUBILEE** MUG *with a white sprigged portrait that has been moulded separately and attached to the blue body. 1897; 3½in high.* **£30–£40**

▽ **PEACE MUG** *produced by the thousand at the end of World War I. The elaborate lithographic transfer print shows the commanders-in-chief of the British sea and land forces. 1919; 4in high.* **£18–£20**

◁ **CHINA MUG** *for George VI's coronation. There was less time to make items for this event, so this is rarer than mugs for Edward VIII, who abdicated. 1937.* **£10–£20**

TEAPOTS

Tea was first drunk for pleasure in ancient China at the time of the Han Dynasty (206–220 BC); until then its uses had been purely medicinal. Tea was initially made in bowls, but pots were introduced in the Song Dynasty (AD 970–1279), and both tea and teapots began to arrive in the West in the 1650s.

The new beverage rapidly became popular and was made in small teapots because tea cost the equivalent of £800 per pound today.

In the late 17th century, China began to export *famille-verte* biscuit porcelain teapots and Imari designs copied from Japan. Though *famille-rose* ware became popular in Britain in the 1740s, demand was greater for the cheaper blue and white teapots, many of which have survived.

▷ **SALT-GLAZE STONEWARE TEAPOT** *by Wedgwood in the form of a Georgian town house. Salt glaze was popular for English tableware, but owing to dangers in the manufacturing process, the factory ceased production in the late 1700s. c.1750; 6in high.* **£1,500**

◁ **MEISSEN ROSE TEAPOT** *The design of this rare piece is based on a Chinese blanc de Chine original; the moulding represents a white rose, with buds for the teapot's feet. Most Meissen flower-encrusted wares date from the 1770s. 1740; 5in high.* **£1,000**

THE CHANGING SHAPE OF THE TEAPOT

CHINESE EXPORT PORCELAIN, 1728

CHELSEA PORCELAIN, MOULDED, 1748

WHIELDON REDWARE, 1750

WORCESTER PORCELAIN, 1775

▷ **"FIRST PERIOD" WORCESTER TEAPOT** *based on a contemporary Chinese* famille-rose *original and painted in enamels and gilding. Worcester pieces made before 1780 used to be called "Dr Wall" after one of the original partners; they are now know as "First Period". 1765; 6½in high.* **£600–£900**

◁△ **UNDERGLAZE BLUE TEAPOT** *in Neo-classical shape. One side displays a house in a park, the other a lady named Sally Sikes. Dated 1781; 5½in high.* **£600–£900**

▷ **CREAMWARE TEAPOT** *painted with a stylized plant design on one side and an inscription on the other. Such messages often appear on gifts that sailors gave to their loved ones before setting sail. The feathery decoration and the scroll handle are Rococo features. 1780; 5in high.* **£300–£500**

NEW HALL PORCELAIN, 1790	WEDGWOOD WHITE STONEWARE, 1820	ROCKINGHAM BONE CHINA, 1830–35	COPELAND EARTHENWARE, 1880

Early 18th-century teapots were globular or pear shaped, but in the 1740s and '50s, during the Rococo period, there was a vogue for eccentric teapots shaped like shells, camels, houses and even fat "Chinamen".

In the mid-18th century the inspiration for many English and French styles was provided by early Chinese teapots, such as those made from Yixing ware (a red stoneware body which supposedly produced the best tea) and *blanc de Chine*, from southeast China.

The 19th century saw a return to globular teapots; Wedgwood's black basalt, "squashed" disc-shaped pots were particularly striking. The Eastern influence produced unusual styles such as bamboo-effect pots, while the Rococo revival in the 1830s resulted in elaborate flower-encrusted pots. Most bizarre, however, were animal-shaped pots that appeared with the advent of majolica in the 1860s.

▷ **BLACK BASALT TEAPOT**
*in a style associated
with Wedgwood,
although this example is
made by an unknown copyist.
Few people collect basalt unless
it is marked Wedgwood – possibly
because of its sombre colour. The
figure on the cover is the biblical
Widow of Zaraphath. 1790s;
5in high.* **£100**

▽ **WHITE STONEWARE TEAPOT**
*made by Clulow and Co. in Fenton,
Staffordshire. The overall design
shows a strong Classical influence.
The moulded details include a
figure standing beside an urn and*

*foliage decorating the handle, top
and spout. The outline is picked
out in a rich blue typical of the
period. 1780–1810; 7in high.* **£400**

◁ **EARTHENWARE TEAPOT**
made by Harley of Lane End and coloured in the "Pratt" palette under a pearlware glaze. It is unstained, which is rare, but the castellation and the swan's head are damaged; in perfect condition the value could be four times as much. 1805; 4in high. **£100**

▷ **REGENCY TEAPOT**
The brightly coloured enamels and gilding used to decorate this well-made piece are typical of many Regency wares. Although its shape follows that of classic silver Regency teapots, there is basketry-style moulding on the sides. 1810–20; 7in high.
£1,200–£1,600

CADOGAN TEAPOT

This teapot style developed from the Chinese peach-shaped wine pot supposedly first used by Lady Cadogan in the late 18th century. It works on the unspillable inkwell principle and is filled through a hole in the underside, with an inner tube that runs to just below the top. This Spode example is rare; pieces by Rockingham are more usual. 1820; 8in high. **£250**

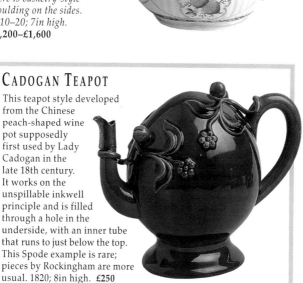

▷ **STAFFORDSHIRE TEAPOT** *made of white stoneware. The cast is of good quality, and the decorative pattern includes stylized palmettes on a seeded ground. Victorian pottery such as this can often be found quite inexpensively. c.1865; 5in high.* **£60**

▽ **MINTON MAJOLICA TEAPOT** *in the shape of a monkey clutching a coconut. The spout is chipped, but otherwise this is an excellent example of the japonaiserie made following the London Exhibition of 1867. The design of the monkey's jacket imitates an embroidered Japanese jacket. 1870; 5in high.* **£700**

◁ **BELLEEK TEA KETTLE** *The design of this piece, called "Grass", is picked out in enamels and lustrous pink. The Belleek factory in County Fermanagh, Northern Ireland, made both tea kettles – which have overhead handles, as here – and teapots with side handles. 1880; 7in high.* **£300**

◁ **HEXAGONAL TEAPOT** *made in Staffordshire of earthenware with restrained blue and black decoration. In the late 19th century, teapots were largely mass produced in almost infinite variety. Despite this, the sheer range of designs makes this a rich period for collectors. Late 19th century; 8in high.* **£25–£35**

▷ **JAPANESE TEAPOT** *This form of pot, made in Seto, has two loops to take a basketwork handle. These pots were made in great numbers and are therefore very inexpensive. c.1920; 3in high.* **£2–£10**

A MEASHAM "BARGE TEAPOT"

This large dated teapot, made in Measham, Derbyshire, has an unusual double spout and a lid in the shape of a tiny teapot. The nickname "barge teapot" originated in the late 19th century, when such pots were owned by bargees in the Staffordshire area. These workers often spent their holidays picking hops and, if money was tight, they walked, taking the teapot with them, instead of catching a train. 1895; 11in high. **£100**

TEA SERVICES

The first tea bowls, saucers and teapots arrived in the West with the first shipments of tea from China. From the mid-18th century, matched porcelain tea sets based on Oriental designs were being produced by continental makers. Full sets comprised a teapot, teapot stand, sugar box and cover, milk jug (sometimes with a lid), slop bowl, bread plates, spoon tray, tea and coffee cups and saucers.

Some of the earliest European tea wares were produced by Meissen, in Saxony, first in a hard red stoneware, and later in white hard-paste porcelain. From the 1740s, finely painted Rococo sets appeared, with some of the finest examples made by the French factory, Sèvres.

In England, from the mid-1740s, tea services were made in soft-paste porcelain by Chelsea, and in the 1760s Wedgwood developed a cream-coloured earthenware he called Queen's Ware, which was popular throughout Europe.

△ **HAND-PAINTED TEA SERVICE**
by Minton, whose early bone-china tablewares rivalled those of other makers such as Spode, Mason and Davenport. This virtually complete set, with botanical decoration, is Minton at its best: each piece carries the famous crossed L mark, with M and the pattern number, here 786 (inset). 1812; Cups 2½in high.
The set **£1,500–£2,000**

▷ **COALPORT TEA SERVICE**
Any elaborate Rococo-revival tea service was once attributed to Rockingham, but research has now disclosed who made what. Pattern numbers can frequently provide the necessary evidence. c.1830; Teapot 7in high. **£1,250**

△ **MEISSEN PART TEA SET** *consisting of tea bowls and saucers and a covered sugar bowl with a floral knop. They are painted with* *figures in German landscapes, probably near Dresden, where the Meissen factory was situated. 1740; Tea bowl 1¾in high.* **£2,500**

◁ **PINK LUSTRE TEA SERVICE** *by Dawson of Sunderland. Although impressed marks are rarely seen on lustre pottery, this example is marked. The panels of figures are transfer printed and hand coloured. 1821; Teapot 5in high.* **£450**

Many English tea services imitated Japanese Kakiemon porcelain in iron-red, blue, yellow and turquoise enamels, as well as Imari patterns of alternating bands of decoration.

When bone china was invented in the early 19th century, great numbers of tea services were made using this fine white translucent porcelain; Spode's hand-painted wares are particularly collectable.

Some of the finest late 19th-century sets are enamelled wares made by Royal Worcester and Copeland. Some sets did not include a teapot, sugar bowl or cream jug; these would have been in silver. A set without these pieces today, therefore, is not necessarily incomplete.

Full tea services command the highest prices. Less dear are incomplete sets which, with at least six pieces, are quite usable.

THE CABARET TEA SET

When morning tea was taken in the bedroom, a variation on the full tea service was used – the "cabaret" set. These usually comprised one or two cups and saucers, a teapot, milk jug, sugar bowl and slop bowl, all on a matching tray.

◁ CABARET, OR "SOLITAIRE", TEA SET *in underglaze blue and bright enamels on Empire-style forms. The best examples of these sets were made by Swansea; this one, however, is by Coalport or Davenport. 1810–15; Teapot 5in high.* £600–£1,000

▷ MINTON MAJOLICA TEA SET *Tea sets of this type are highly sought after, since they rarely survive intact. The pieces are marked with the maker's name, the pattern and mould number, the potter's mark and the date code. Date codes in a set commonly varied by a few years. 1872–74; Teapot 5in high.* £3,000

△ **DOULTON STONEWARE TEA SET**
with moulded decoration. Initially,
Doulton specialized in stoneware
drainpipes, but produced art wares
after 1860. Were this set complete –
one cover does not match – it would
be worth half as much again. 1879;
Teapot 4in high. The set **£250**.

△ **"JACOBETHAN"-STYLE TEA SET**
Each of the pieces is slip cast as an
oak-beamed cottage in a curious
hybrid of the Elizabethan and
Jacobean styles in architecture.
Such pieces were popular in the
early years of the 20th century.
c.1920; 2½–4½in high. **£60–£80**

△ **JAPANESE EGGSHELL SERVICE**
Millions of these sets were exported
from c.1900 to c.1939. Most were
thinly potted and crudely painted,
often within a transfer or stencilled
guide, as here. This set was
probably made in Kutani. 1920;
Teapot 9in high. Each piece **£2–£3**

COFFEE SERVICES

Before tea became popular, coffee and chocolate were the most common non-alcoholic drinks, both in the home and in the coffee houses which had sprung up all over Europe.

The habit of drinking coffee spread from the Near East, and the first coffee pots looked like Turkish wine jugs, but the shape soon changed to resemble that of the teapot, with a cover and, usually, a handle opposite the spout. Chocolate pots looked much like coffee pots, except for a hole in the lid through which a stick, or *molinet*, was inserted to stir up the contents.

THE MEISSEN INFLUENCE

The formula for hard-paste porcelain, first made in Europe at Meissen in 1710, was coveted by all the other makers of ceramics. Although the secret was jealously guarded, artisans at the factory left to work elsewhere, taking their knowledge with them, and within 20 years imitations of Meissen porcelain were being made throughout the Germanic countries, in France and in Britain.

LUDWIGSBURG COFFEE POT, *inspired by Meissen. 1760s; 9in.* **£1000–£1,500**

MEISSEN CHOCOLATE POT *with typical ear-shaped handle. 1740s; 8in high.* **£2,000**

▷ **PORCELAIN COFFEE SET** *in Empire style, with well- painted views and gilding in good condition, probably made in Paris. The set consists of 14 cups, a small coffee pot and a milk jug; originally it there would also have been a covered sugar bowl and plates but not necessarily saucers. c.1820.* **Set as it is £500**

▷ **MILK JUG AND COVER** *of a shape often included in tea and coffee sets and made at Caughley, Shropshire. The factory, set up in 1772 and taken over by Coalport in 1799, made mainly blue and white wares imitating those from Worcester, but also some fine polychrome pieces. This jug was painted and gilded in the London studio of James Giles, the foremost decorator of the day. 1775; 5in high.* **£1,200–£1,500**

▽ **NORITAKE COFFEE SET** *in eggshell porcelain. It is unusually well decorated in a design based on a Chinese textile. Thousands of these sets were exported by the Japanese, and the extreme thinness of the porcelain has, paradoxically, ensured their survival, since people were afraid to use them. 1920; Coffee pot 7in high.* **£100**

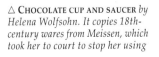

△ **CHOCOLATE CUP AND SAUCER** *by Helena Wolfsohn. It copies 18th-century wares from Meissen, which took her to court to stop her using* *their designs and the AR monogram of Augustus Rex, Elector of Saxony, the founder of the factory. 1880; Cup 2¾in high.* **£40–£60**

CUPS & SAUCERS

The origins of the tea cup lie in the handleless *chawan,* or tea bowl, used in traditional Buddhist tea ceremonies. European examples were first made, in silver, in the early 1600s, and in ceramics later in the century.

Cups with handles appeared in the 1770s, and the traditional tea-cup shape of a wide, shallow bowl with a handle was established by 1760. Decoration on English cups was frequently a combination of hand painting and transfer-printed patterns, but hand painting continued for both the best and worst wares. On shallow mid-Victorian cups, the decoration was often on the inside, where it was more easily seen, with only a simple gilded motif on the outside.

Tea cups are ideal for collectors on a limited budget, since good-quality items can be found plentifully and inexpensively.

THE TEA BOWL

◁ **JAPANESE CHAWAN,** *or tea bowl, of traditional deep form. The low-fired bricklike body is deep salmon pink and grey. It is signed by the noted maker Ryonyu. Mid-19th century; 3in high.* **£600–£800**

▷ **CHELSEA TEA BOWL AND SAUCER** *Sets are often broken up nowadays and the pieces sold as cups and saucers or as trios. c.1770; Saucer 4in diameter.* **£80–£120**

◁ **TEA BOWL** *made in Suffolk at the Lowestoft factory. Early examples are in underglaze blue; later pieces employed enamel colouring, particularly red, as here. 1880–85; 1½in high.* **£80**

△ **CUP, TEA BOWL AND SAUCER**
This set, referred to as a "trio", is
decorated with a black overglaze
transfer scene (called "l'Amour")
engraved by Robert Hancock, who
developed the technique at
Worcester. Overglaze is applied on
top of the glaze and is thus very
prone to wear, which affects the
price. 1775; Saucer 5in. **£250–£350**

▷ **"FIRST PERIOD" OCTAGONAL
TEA CUP** made by Worcester with
a scroll handle and typically
restrained use of Kakiemon-style
decoration in a famille-verte
palette. 1753–55; 2¼in high.
£1,000

△ **TEA CUP AND SAUCER** by Barr,
Flight & Barr, who worked at
Worcester in the Regency period.
The pieces are bat printed (a
variation of transfer printing
which gives the most superior
reproduction) in black with
Classical subjects on a simulated
gold-marbled ground. The
impressed mark (above) may be
accompanied by written marks
on larger pieces. 1804–13;
Cup 2½in high. **£250–£350**

▷ **Tea cup and saucer** *made by H. & R. Daniel, with the pattern number 4581. The decoration, of birds on tree branches, at the bottom of the cup (not visible) and the burnished gilding on a deep blue ground, is typical of late Regency wares. The cup is one of 12 belonging to a set now comprising a teapot, 2 plates, 8 coffee cups, 11 saucers, a slop bowl and a milk jug. 1830; Saucer 4in.* Set **£300–£400**; Cup and saucer **£15–£20**

△ **Giant Staffordshire cup and saucer,** *transfer-printed with the Chinese-influenced Willow pattern. It has a typically bright and brassy mercury-gilt line border. These cups were not simply ornaments, but were used by factory workers or miners, who often consumed several pints of tea after returning home from a shift. 1880; 4in high.* **£35**

▷ **Shamrock-pattern tea cup** *The Belleek tea service from which this item derives has 12 cups and saucers, teapot, hot water jug, sugar bowl and milk jug. Belleek tea services carry a mark to reassure owners that the extraordinarily thin teapot walls will not crack. The pattern is still made today. 1895; Saucer 5½in wide.* **£40–£60**

△ **JAPANESE CUP AND SAUCER,** *with a decorative theme of large butterflies on a deep blue ground, made by Noritake for the European* market. *Cloisonné was frequently similarly decorated, as were pieces from Wedgwood. Early 1900s; Saucer 5½in.* **£40**

◁ **"LIMPET" DESIGN TEA SET** *Part of a Belleek set that was first made in about 1880 and produced until 1989; this one carries a black "third period" (1926–46) mark. When, as here, they lack the teapot, sets may be bought by dealers, who sell the pieces separately. c.1930; Plate 12in. The set* **£400**

▷ **ART DECO CUP AND SAUCER** *from a breakfast set for four people, complete with teapot, creamer and sugar bowl. The decoration on this piece follows the Art Deco style prevalent at the time, and, although such sets are relatively inexpensive at the moment, their value is increasing steadily. 1930; 3in high.* **£10–£15**

TABLEWARES

The earliest English soft-paste
porcelain dinner services, made from
the mid-18th century, are today virtually
impossible to find complete.
Indeed, single pieces of these tablewares,
made only for the wealthy, are still
out of the financial reach of the average
collector. But once greater numbers
of wares were made for an expanding
middle class, the choice becomes vast.
From the 1760s, creamware
dominated the dining table, to be
succeeded toward the end of the century
by pearlware, also a Josiah Wedgwood
development; and early in the 19th
century, durable ironstone appeared.
As with tea and coffee wares,
services are often broken to suit
collectors and the important interior
decorators' market.
As a result, more sought-after
pieces, such as a pair of sauce tureens
with covers and stands, could fetch up
to £1,000, whereas a plate from
the same service may
make only £30–£50.

DINNER SERVICES

Silver, pewter or wood were commonly used for tablewares in Europe until the 1500s, and such ceramic tablewares as there were consisted of individual bowls or plates, or perhaps a run of several in the same shape and pattern.

Plates and dishes in tin-glazed earthenware, known as Delft in Holland and delftware in England, were made throughout the 17th and 18th centuries, but they chipped easily. Josiah Wedgwood's lead-glazed cream-ware, which he named Queen's Ware, produced from the mid-18th century, was more satisfactory, but large, elaborate dinner services as such were not made until later in the century.

The grandest of these contained soup and meat plates, dishes in various sizes for meat and fish, vegetable dishes, and tureens for both soup and sauces. Sometimes plates and dishes for dessert were also included.

△ **CHELSEA CLARET-GROUND PART SERVICE** *Chelsea porcelain is divided into four periods, indicated by factory marks. An incised triangle (1745–49) was followed until 1752 by an anchor, moulded in relief on a pad. The red anchor marks a period (1752–57) when many of the best-known Chelsea pieces were made. The plates here, with ornate floral designs, rich ground colour and fine gilding inspired by Sèvres wares, are typical of the gold anchor period (1757–69). c.1765; Plate 12in.*
Pair of plates **£800–£1,200**

△ **VIENNA PART DINNER SERVICE**
By bribing Meissen workers to defect to it, the long-lived Vienna factory (1718 to the early 1800s) was the second in Europe to achieve hard-paste porcelain. The similarity to Meissen wares is evident in the painting of the European flowers and in the palette, while the moulding shows a strong Rococo influence. c.1765; Oval dish 15in long. Pair of dishes **£400–£600**

△ **COALPORT PART DINNER SERVICE**
These items, from a set of more than 100 remaining pieces, are decorated with a bold Japanese pattern in underglaze blue and gilt, with red, yellow and brown flowerheads and trailing honeysuckle. The tureens have gilt lion's head handles and lion finials on the lids. Coalport produced more dinner services than any other factory at this time. c.1810. **£5,000–£7,000**

PLATES & DISHES

The Chinese discovered how to make porcelain in the 7th century, but it was not until the 14th century that they discovered that black cobalt oxide under the glaze turned blue when fired. At first, blue and white pieces were all made for export to the the Middle East, and it was only in the 16th century that quantities of blue and white porcelain, known as "kraak", were sent to Europe.

After the establishment of the Qing Dynasty in 1644, the export of porcelain to the West became a flood. Some of these wares were armorials, dinner

◁ **KRAAK CHARGER** *In the mid-16th century, a style of decoration on Chinese porcelain known as kraak (after the ships, or carracks, in which it was exported) became popular in Europe. All kraak pieces were thinly potted and painted with a central design and a border of flowers, knots and precious objects. c.1600; 19in.* **£2,000–£3,000**

▷ **MEAT DISHES** *from a Chinese export dinner service. Many such platters have survived, and their shape and style were also widely copied. c.1760; 14in, 13in long.* Each **£120**

◁ **CHINESE PLATE** *in underglaze blue and white, enriched in iron-red and gold. The colour was probably added in Europe, a process known as clobbering. Plates like this fetch less than those with only blue decoration. Late 1600s; 9in.* **£100**

services painted in *famille-rose* and *famille-verte* enamels to the order of European families.

Cheaper blue and white wares continued to dominate the market, however, and the palette was copied in Europe, first in the Dutch tin-glazed earthenware known as Delft, and then in the ubiquitously produced English delftware. The popularity of such wares is undiminished today.

△ **UNUSUAL CHINESE EXPORT PLATE** *painted in a refined style in underglaze blue, iron-red and other enamels. The curious fan shape may have been a family crest. 1720–40; 10in.* **£300–£500**

△ **FAMILLE-VERTE DISH** *The decoration on this shallow dish, with its predominantly leaf-green colouring, is more to Chinese taste than is usual in export ware. 1700; 13in.* **£1,000–£1,500**

ARMORIAL WARES

In the 1700s, English families sent coats of arms to China to be painted on dinner services, sometimes with amusing mistakes, although the quality of the work was usually high.

△ **THE CREST** *of the Vernons of Hanbury Hall has here been rendered as a girl with a sheaf of rice. 1730.* **£1,500–£2,000**

△ **PLATE** *with the owner's labels wrongly incorporated into the banner beneath the arms. 1740; 8¼in.* **£1,200**

△ **MEAT DISH** *in underglaze blue with a crest, the initials "IK" and a motto in English. 1780s; 18in.* **£300–£600**

In contrast to the flourishing trade in ceramics with China, that with Japan was limited, particularly after access was all but closed to the West in the 1630s. Of those wares that did reach Europe, Kakiemon porcelain was the most prized, but its influence never matched that of Chinese wares.

It was not until 1713 that true hard-paste porcelain was made in Europe, at the Meissen factory outside Dresden, and it was some time before the formula was spread by defecting workmen to factories in Vienna and, eventually, France.

Although soft-paste porcelain was produced by many factories in Britain, among the best of which was Chelsea, true hard-paste porcelain, or bone china, was not made until 1780. And several factories, most notably Wedgwood, continued to make superb earthenwares, such as creamware and pearlware.

▷ **RARE KAKIEMON PLATE** *made at Arita in Japan. Kakiemon is one of the most coveted types of Japanese porcelain. It usually had skilfully applied multicoloured translucent enamelling; very little was decorated in blue only. Such plates are worth more sold individually than as part of a set. 1720; 8in.*
£1,500–£2,000

◁ **ENGLISH DELFTWARE PLATE** *made at Wincanton, Somerset. The design shows a lady in a garden, with sponged-on trees in a manganese oxide dye, which produces the dark plum colour. The plate is in fine condition and is most unusual in that it depicts a European scene; most of this type of delftware shows Chinese scenes. c.1745–50; 9in.*
£500–£600

◁ **CHELSEA PLATE** *This fine piece of porcelain from the red anchor period (1752–57) demonstrates the way in which painters created designs to cover up imperfections that frequently occurred during firing, sometimes giving the decoration a slightly haphazard look. Here, the greengage covers a rough patch on the surface and a beetle disguises a firing hole. 8in.*
£700–£1,000

ROYAL PLATES

Russian royalty were enthusiastic patrons of the great ceramics factories in France, Germany and England, and pieces with royal connections are much sought after today.

▽ **SÈVRES PORCELAIN PLATES** *based on Sèvres designs first produced c.1775. They were made for the Russian royal yacht, and one of the plates bears the mark for Nicholas II, 1891, the other the mark for Alexander III, 1903. Both plates 9½in.* The pair **£3,000**

△ **"FROG" PLATE** *from a dinner service ordered from Wedgwood by Catherine the Great of Russia for the Grenouillière Palace in St. Petersburg (grenouille is the French for frog). 1773–74; 9in.* **£12,000–£15,000**

▷ **WEDGWOOD PEARLWARE PLATE**
Josiah Wedgwood introduced this
fine white earthenware in 1779
as a development of his "Queen's
Ware", which was itself a refined
form of creamware that could be
easily potted and decorated. The
blue tint of the pearlware glaze
made it nearer to the Chinese
originals. c.1810; 9in. **£40**

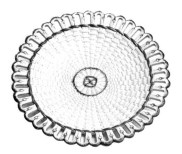

△ **PEARLWARE PLATES,** *two of a set*
of six which were probably made
in Yorkshire and painted with
exotic birds by young girls in the
factory. Such plates are much
sought after by collectors. c.1820;
9½in. The set **£1,500–£2,000**

WILLOW PATTERN DESIGN

Probably the most famous of
all Staffordshire transfer-
printed designs, Willow
Pattern was inspired by
Chinese blue and white
ware. This plate, by
Dillwyn & Co. of
Swansea, includes
all the usual features:
five stylized trees; a
boat; a zigzag fence; a
pair of birds and figures on
a bridge. 1820–30; 10in. **£50**

CHILDREN'S PLATES

Pottery wares made for children are also becoming popular with collectors. They tended not to last long and it is rare to find them in good condition. These plates, printed with scenes from the biblical story of Joseph, are of better quality than usual. The moulded border is typical of the Swansea Pottery. 1820–30; 6½in. Each £100

◁ **MINTON PLATE** *from a dessert service. The tradition of fine painting on bone-china dessert services was maintained in the 1870s by French artists such as Antoine Boullemier. This Sèvres-style scene, within a turquoise border, is typical of his work.* 1875; 8in. **£200–£300**

▷ **PLATE** *decorated with a steam locomotive after the artist and graphic designer Eric Ravilious (1903–42), who produced several such images in a "Travel" series for Wedgwood in the 1930s. Pieces decorated with Ravilious's designs are much sought after.* 1936–40; 10in. **£120**

COMMEMORATIVE WARES

Makers of ceramics have always been quick to produce special commemorative pieces with an instant appeal to the buying public. As well as mugs and jugs, fine plates have been made, which form a rewarding field for the collector with historical interests.

Among the earliest are the delftware plates commemorating Charles II's restoration to the English throne in 1660, and mementos of royal occasions have remained a constant.

There has also, over the centuries, been a steady flow of plates and bowls marking events of public interest, such as battles, which are highly collectable.

◁ **ENGLISH DELFTWARE PLATE,** *probably made by the factory at Lambeth in London. This entertaining plate, of interest to devotees of ballooning as well as collectors, commemorates the ascent in 1784 in a hot-air balloon by Vincent Lunardi. 1785; 9in.* **£800–£1,000**

▷ **SCOTTISH PEARLWARE** *porridge bowl inscribed "Waterloo". It was, possibly, made at the Portobello factory in Leith and is extremely rare. c.1815; 5in wide.* **£400–£600**

◁ **POTTERY BOWL** *made at the Portobello factory almost exactly 100 years later than the bowl above. This patriotic piece, with the words "It's a long way to Tipperary" and showing marching soldiers, crowns and flags, perhaps commemorates the Battle of the Somme. c.1916; 7in across.* **£60–£80**

ROYAL COMMEMORATIVE PLATES

▷ **ENGLISH DELFTWARE CHARGER** *showing William, who reigned alone (1693–1704) after Mary's death. c.1700; 13½in.* **£4,000–£6,000**

▷ **QUEEN VICTORIA GOLDEN JUBILEE PLATE** *Similar plates were made to celebrate her Diamond Jubilee 10 years later. 1887; 9in.* **£40–£60**

◁ **DELFT PLATE** *made in Holland for the English market at about the time of William and Mary's coronation in 1689. Late 17th century; 11in.* **£2,000–£3,000**

◁ **PLATE** *made in support of Queen Caroline after she was locked out of Westminster Abbey during the coronation of George IV. 1820; 3½in.* **£150–£250**

◁ **PARAGON CHINA PLATE** *in a design made for the coronation of Edward VIII and adapted for his brother George VI. 1937; 8in.* **£150–£200**

BOWLS

Since the earliest times, bowls have been used for storing, cooking and eating. Bowls were among the grave goods in ancient China, and 18th-century blue and white bowls were among the earliest Chinese ceramics to reach the West.

By the 1700s demand was great for Oriental export pieces, often painted with designs requested by western clients. In Holland and in England, in an attempt to capture some of this trade, earthenware bowls were made that closely followed Oriental styles and decoration, although commemorative themes were also popular.

Because they are difficult to display, bowls are often cheaper than plates: they cannot be wall-mounted, and any interior decoration is hidden if they are used to hold fruit or flowers, say, or pot-pourri.

◁ **DUTCH DELFT BOWL** *painted with Chinese landscape scenes. Delft wares were soft, and pieces were easily damaged, this being no exception: it has a large hairline crack and a chip on the foot, halving its value. 1710; 14in wide.* **£300**

▷ **DUTCH TIN-GLAZED EARTHENWARE BOWL** *English examples may be difficult to distinguish from the Dutch. Although made some 20 years later than the one above, the shape is comparable. 1731; 15in wide.* **£3,000**

◁ **STAFFORDSHIRE POTTERY BOWL** *transfer printed with a band of roses and a country scene in a rich blue. The subject matter is attractive – scenes showing a rural way of life are popular. c.1840; 9in wide.* Cracked **£30**; In perfect condition **£80**

◁ **CREAMWARE BOWL** *An uncommon piece, probably made in Yorkshire. The surface of the plain earthenware body has been decorated in brown and blue with liquid clay slip which has been "joggled" to resemble agate. c.1780; 7in wide.* **£150–£250**

▷ **SUNDERLAND LUSTRE BOWL** *with transfer prints of the cast-iron bridge over the River Wear (represented on this pottery throughout the 19th century), various nautical rhymes and a picture of the Sailor's Farewell. It has the somewhat hastily decorated look of a middle-period piece. c.1850; 10in wide.* **£300**

◁ **JAPANESE IMARI BOWL** *typically decorated in underglaze blue, iron-red and gilding and, here, with additional green and yellow enamels. The shape of the bowl is typical of wares made for export during the 19th century and into the 20th. 1900; 10in wide.* **£100–£150**

▷ **FRENCH FAIENCE BOWL** *The base of this good-quality decorative bowl, with its brightly enamelled flowers, bears the mark of Le Nove. Production of this type of ware has continued at the factory from the 18th century to the present. 1920s; 14in wide.* **£300–£400**

TUREENS & SAUCEBOATS

In Britain in the 18th century, entertaining among an increasingly large middle class led to the introduction of a wide range of dinner wares. Among them were large covered tureens for soup and vegetables and small tureens and sauceboats – oval boat-shaped dishes on a foot – for sweet and savoury sauces.

The shapes of ceramic pieces followed those of contemporary silver, and porcelain tureens were often equipped with their own stands and many even had accompanying ladles.

Early silver sauceboats had handles at each end and lips on either side, but their porcelain counterparts usually had the handle opposite the lip. Sauceboats generally had a stand and, as with tureens, where this is missing, the value is reduced.

△ TUREEN, COVER AND STAND *painted in blue and white with peonies and chrysanthemums. Both the shape and decoration are typical* of Chinese wares made expressly for export to European markets during the 18th century. 1750; Stand 16in wide. **£1,500–£2,000**

◁ SAUCEBOAT *with moulded swags painted in enamels; a rare item from Benjamin Lund's Bristol factory, taken over by Worcester in 1752. c.1751; 8in long.* **£2,00–£3,000**

▷ RARE PLYMOUTH SAUCEBOAT *by William Cookworthy, the Quaker chemist who developed the formula for true porcelain in Britain. c.1770; 3in high.* **£500**

△ **SAUCE TUREEN, COVER AND LADLE** *made at Worcester and painted with landscape panels and fruit in a pattern known as "The* Lord Henry Thynne" after the eldest son of the then Marquis of Bath. With the stand, the price would be double. c.1775; 5in long. **£2,500**

◁ **SOUP TUREEN** in Mason's ironstone. It was transfer printed in greyish black with Imari-style flowers, which were then hand painted. Since enamels and the gilding matured at different temperatures, a piece might be fired several times. c.1820; 7in high. **£500**

△ **WORCESTER SAUCE TUREEN** which owes its origins to Sèvres. The overlapping scales and the floral panels are typical of Worcester at this date. There is a pseudo-Chinese mark on the base. c.1770; 9in wide. **£1,500–£2,000**

DESSERT SERVICES

In the mid-18th century, it became fashionable at the end of a meal to have dessert: fruit, nuts, ices, custard and so on. Special dessert services were being produced and, since they did not have to withstand the rough treatment of the meat course, they tended to be the richest and most impressive services of the meal.

Dessert services usually consisted of baskets and dishes for fruit and sweetmeats, bowls, tureens and plates that were a little smaller than dinner plates. The decoration included landscapes, flowers and birds, often with elaborate gilding. Well-painted sets with yellow borders are especially valuable, since the colour was so hard to fire.

△ **DERBY DESSERT SERVICE** *The factory at Derby became renowned for high-quality decoration on porcelain. In the late 18th century and early 19th, botanical painting was especially fashionable, with specimen flowers depicted in great*

detail and in vivid colours. In this dessert service in the style of John Brewer, one of the skilled artists working for the factory, the back of each piece bears both the common and scientific names of the flower. c.1800. **£35,000–£45,000**

MINTON FRUIT DISH

In 1793, Thomas Minton set up a pottery in Stoke-on-Trent that was to become one of the great names in British ceramics. By the early 19th century, he was making high-quality bone-china tablewares in a wide range of painted, printed and gilded patterns. The design on this dish for fruit and nuts, part of a large dessert service, is loosely based on a design found on ceramics from the Far East. 1805; 10in wide. **£200–£300**

MINTON MARKS

| PAINTED, 1800–30 | MINTON & HOLLINS, PRINTED, 1845–68 | c.1850 ONWARD | PRINTED, 1860–69 |

◁ **CENTRE DISH** *from a dessert service made by W. & R. Ridgway. This maker's wares usually have a solid ground of rather dull grey, but the marbled ground here has been stipple printed (a mass-production technique) in an attempt to copy contemporary hand-painted botanical services. c.1830; 13½in long.* **£250–£300**

▷ **SPODE BAT-PRINTED DISH** *with gilding. Bat printing was a form of transfer printing in which the design was printed in oil on a flexible sheet, or bat, of gelatine and glue. This was pressed into the porcelain and dusted with black powder before firing. 1810–15; 11in long.* **£100**

▽ **BASE MARK FOR**
1807–13 *The most technically proficient Worcester porcelain was made from 1792 to 1840, when the factory was controlled by Thomas Flight and the two Martin Barrs (father and son). The marks vary during this period, but always carry the three names.*

△ **WORCESTER DESSERT DISH**
The bold and unusual design on this dish, originally part of a large set, uses Gothic features, such as the stylized oak leaves, within a Japanese Imari-style pattern.
1808; 8in square. **£100–£150**

BARR FLIGHT & BARR
Royal Por elainWorks
WORCESTER

London-House
N.1 Coventry Street

▷ **SPODE PORCELAIN DISH** *which was originally part of a large service. Typically for the time, it has a gilt border and is painted with a limodorum, which would have been copied from a botanical book or periodical. 1815; 12in long.* **£600**

▽ **PARIS PORCELAIN** *at its best. One plate with a well-painted Italian landscape and gilt border in Neo-classical style, the other, by Dihl & Guerhard, with an auricula and fine gilt border. Both c.1800; (l) 9in, (r) 9½in.* **£500 each**

IRONSTONE SERVICE

In 1813, Charles James Mason patented ironstone, a hard white earthenware, and all pieces bear the name (*below right*). This dessert service, which would have contained more than 30 pieces, dates from the early years and is typical of the wares from Mason's factory. The forms, derived from silver designs, have been exaggerated: the wave to the rim of the fruit stand and the scallops on the dish are much bolder than any other maker produced, and the Chinese-style floral decoration is flamboyant (*see detail*). c.1820; Fruit stand £400–£600/Dish £300

OTHER
DOMESTIC WARES

Apart from the usual dinner wares,
the 18th century saw the introduction
of a wide range of additional more
or less functional pieces. Many of these
are no longer in use and have now made
their way into the collector's cabinet.
The Victorians continued the lack
of squeamishness their forefathers
displayed and had no qualms
about making a game pie dish draped
with dead rabbits and pheasants or
a fish dish with highly naturalistic
mackerel forming the handle.
Less disturbingly, they revelled in
objects that suggested their function:
a honey pot in the form of a skep, a jam
pot like a loaf of bread and a cow's head
cheese dish. In the field of domestic
wares, the tyro collector can put together
a large and varied selection without
overstretching himself – the field is vast
and there is a range of prices from a
few pounds to several thousands.

BASKETS & SWEETMEAT DISHES

Apart from dinner wares, many manufacturers made specialist pieces for the table. One such item was the ceramic basket, sometimes with a single overarching handle, that was intended to hold fruit, nuts or sweetmeats.

A typical example was the chestnut basket, made in the 18th century when roasted chestnuts were often served after a meal. Creamware pieces, made by Wedgwood and at Leeds, were moulded and then pierced, their fragile structure making them exceedingly prone to damage.

Ornate Rococo shells or leaves were popular shapes for sweetmeat dishes, which were usually smaller than baskets.

▷ **WORCESTER CHESTNUT BASKET,** *transfer printed as were most such baskets. They have survived in fair numbers but are often damaged, in which event they sell for £100 or less. 1770; 9½in wide.* **£450**

◁ **REGENCY WORCESTER BASKET** *with overlapping moulded gilt leaves, a popular motif also used on Rockingham porcelain. The central scene shows a peasant family in front of a Malvern landscape (as titled on the reverse). The handle has been restored, greatly reducing the value. 1815; 10in wide.* **£800**

▷ **SWEETMEAT DISH** *(one of a pair) in the form of a child playing cymbals beside a shell. The black and gilt base with a "key" pattern is an unusual feature. It was made by Moore Bros., whose designs were closely modelled on those of Minton. 1880; 6in high.* **£150**

△ **BELLEEK BASKET** *The piece has been straw moulded to give a wicker effect, and is decorated with applied flowers and leaves.* *It would have been impractical in use and so would have been a poor seller, hence its rarity. 1900; 6in wide.* **£300**

▷ **"RATHMORE" PATTERN BASKET** *This Belleek design was first made in 1904, and has been in production ever since. The fine "net" effect, typical of the factory, is effected only with great skill. The handles and feet imitate coral. 1990; 11in wide.* **£2,300**

◁ **WEMYSS EGG BASKET** *made for Thomas Goode and Sons, the main dealers in Wemyss ware. The pottery was popular with the gentry in the early 20th century. Its soft, absorbent body was easily damaged and stained and good examples are at a premium. 1900; 7in high* **£1,500**

HOUSEHOLD ITEMS

Ceramics, being generally inexpensive, durable and easily washed, are ideal for utilitarian wares. The original buyer could have pieces that were decorative as well as functional; now, divorced from use, they have become collector's items.

The antiques market is not static and there are sudden bursts of enthusiasm for a newly recognized field: cheese dishes and biscuit barrels are newcomers to the collecting world. Among the best of these uncharted buys are the millions of Chinese blue and white export plates of the second half of the 18th century, which are still relatively inexpensive.

◁ **BUTTER DISH** *One of a pair, this underglaze blue and white butter dish was made in China and exported to the West. The shell shape came from contemporary silver designs. c.1750; 5in wide.* The pair **£600–£800**

▷ **DERBY BUTTER TUB** *The enamel painting on this Derby piece is of good quality. The fine decoration, unusual shape and excellent condition all increase the value. c.1760; 5in wide.* **£1,500–£2,000**

◁ **NOVELTY JAM POT** *The cottage-loaf shape of this Royal Worcester jam pot reflects the Victorian taste for novelty food ceramics which had a visual link with the food they contained. 1900; 6in high.* **£150–£200**

△ **TWO SALTS** *The Chinese export salt (left), dating from the 1740s, was painted in the* famille-rose *palette. That on the right, made in Hungary in the 1890s, replicates armorial pieces of the 1740s. It was fired upside down leaving the top rim unglazed, a flaw disguised by the gilt border. Both 3in wide.* Left **£100–£120**; right **£60–£80**

◁ **NOVELTY CHEESE DISH** *Made in the shape of a cow's head, this English earthenware cheese dish dates from the late Victorian period. c.1895; 7in high.* **£300**

COLLECTION OF JAPANESE JARS

These three amusing jars and covers were made in Japan during the 1920s and '30s. They are the work of two companies, the Maritomo Toki Company of Seto City and the Kahuhon Toki Company of Yokkaichi City. 2in–4in high. The group **£60–£90**

POT-POURRI DISHES

Containers made for pot-pourri, a fragrant mixture of spices and petals used to scent the air, were popular from the mid-18th century. The delftware bowl (*top*), made in the 1750s, is 8 inches wide. The slight damage barely affects its value of £1,000–£1,200. The shape of the lower dish, made at Wedgwood *c.*1815 using the famous *rosso antico* (red stoneware) body, was taken from a Greek *krater,* or bowl for mixing wine and water. It is 13½ inches wide and would fetch £300–£500 at auction.

▷ **JASPER DIP CANDLESTICKS**
One of Wedgwood's most popular innovations, jasperware is a hard, smooth, unglazed stoneware stained with metallic oxides. Originally, the clay itself was stained, but to cut costs, from 1777 the wares were given just an outer coat of colour by dipping them. In 1854, "solid" jasper was reintroduced. These attractively simple candlesticks are less popular than those that are more elaborately decorated. 1840; 9in high. **£200–£300**

◁ **SLIPWARE KNIFEBOX**
A light-coloured slip, or liquid clay, was used to contrast with the dark glaze on this knifebox. It was made around the Halifax area in the Yorkshire potteries in the mid-19th century. 11in long. **£150–£200**

▷ **MEISSEN-STYLE TEA CANISTER**
*Workers from the factory took the
Meissen style of decoration and
the formula for hard-paste porcelain
to factories in Vienna, Italy and
elsewhere in Germany. One of these,
Höchst, made this fine canister. Its
value would be double if it had its
lid. 1770s; 3½in high.* **£1,000**

◁ **STAFFORDSHIRE TEA JAR** *Made
of creamware in the late 18th
century, this small jar is marked
"Bohea", which is black tea of
rather low quality since it was the
last crop of the season. The fact
that the jar has sustained some
damage is reflected in its value.
c.1780; 4in high.* **£120–£150**

PRATTWARE SNUFFBOX

Named after a prominent
Staffordshire potting family,
prattware is a creamware
body typically decorated in
underglaze green, ochre and
brown. This unusual snuffbox,
made in Yorkshire, is based on

the enamelled pieces made at
Bilston, Staffordshire. Pictured
on one end is a dog on a
cushion; on the other, which
unscrews to take the snuff, is
the inscription " E.O. 1795".
2in high. **£1,000**

Vessels for storing and serving alcohol have existed for thousands of years; the earliest, such as ancient Greek wine jars, are now museum pieces. Highly prized, however, are German stoneware tankards and jugs, made since the Middle Ages, and English delftware wine bottles from the 17th century; later copies are plentiful but less valuable.

In about 1700, the vogue for drinking punch – a mixture of alcohol and spices – led to specialist punch bowls. The drink was mixed in these vessels and served using a ladle. Both delftware and Chinese examples are sought after and the best can make thousands of pounds at auction.

Also of interest to collectors are the decorative barrels used in Victorian public houses or bars for storing spirits or beer.

BARRELS FOR SPIRITS

SALT-GLAZED STONEWARE BRANDY BARREL *The decoration takes the form of a knight on horseback and a lion couchant. Although many barrels survive, rarely is one found in such good condition. c.1830; 10½in.* **£600**

◁ **FAMILLE-ROSE PUNCH BOWL** *in the palette known as Mandarin, which included a purple-pink. Pieces decorated with European subjects, such as this hunting scene, are usually more expensive than those with Chinese designs. c.1760; 11in wide.* **£1,800–£2,000**

▷ **PEARLWARE PUNCH BOWL** *transfer printed with Romantic rustic scenes of medieval castles, ruins and cottages. This piece was made by one of the Staffordshire factories. c.1820; 11in wide.* **£120–£150**

EARTHENWARE GIN BARREL
*Although these wares were
generally unmarked, this well-
decorated example bears the
Belleek factory mark and date,
which make it more desirable.
1877; 11in high.* **£500–£700**

△ **GERMAN STEIN, OR TANKARD,**
*made of porcelain and decorated
with a landscape reminiscent of
Dutch Delft. The base bears a
lithophane – a low relief which
produces a tonal picture when it
is held to the light. 1890–1910;
8in high.* **£100**

▷ **"REMBRANDTWARE" JUG** *made
at Doulton by the studio head,
Charles Noke, who was noted
for his use of experimental
glazes on useful and domestic
wares. It advertises Dewar's
whisky. Pieces such as this are
becoming increasingly collectable.
1910–20; 7in high.* **£150**

BEDROOM & TOILET WARES

It was not until after World War II that the majority of houses in Britain had indoor bathrooms. Before that time, most people's morning wash entailed using a basin of water poured from a ewer.

The simplest bedroom sets included a matching ewer, basin and soap dish, although more elaborate sets also had a sponge bowl, toothbrush holder and two chamber pots, which were kept in a bedside cupboard, known as a commode.

Since these sets are now redundant, they are often split up. In America, it is rumoured that the chamber pots are sometimes used as punch bowls.

△ **SUNDERLAND BASIN AND EWER**
The pink lustre borders on these pieces are typical of Sunderland wares. They have been in production on and off since the early 19th century. The quality of the potting, the prints and the pink lustre varies according to the date at which they were made. Reproductions made in the 1920s are the most deceptive.

This set is decorated with transfer prints of the bridge over the River Wear on the outside of the basin and poems on a watery theme inside the basin and on the jug. c.1840; Basin 12in wide/Jug 9in high. **£300**

△ **BELLEEK BEDROOM SET** *Although Belleek wares are popular, plain pieces are less sought after. If these were decorated, the value would be double, but without the factory mark their value would be under £40. c.1870; Jug 9in high.* **£150**

▷ **EWER AND BASIN** *Made in Staffordshire in the late 19th century, this ewer and matching basin were transfer printed. The transfer-printed design was hand coloured, often by children, and was far cheaper than hand painting. c.1890; Jug 15in high.* **£150–£200**

◁ **EWER AND BASIN** *transfer printed with flowers in underglaze blue. The Gater, Hall & Co. factory where it was made changed hands – and thus marks – several times, and dating can, therefore, be precise. 1914; Jug 14in high.* **£50**

▷ **EARTHENWARE BEDROOM SET** *This set, by Thomas Lawrence of Longton, a small factory at Stoke-on-Trent, was decorated using both hand painting and spraying. The jars and chamber pot (not shown) enhance the value of the set. c.1925; Jug 15in high.* **£100**

CHAMBER POT

Hand painted with orange and yellow daffodils over a transfer, this Doulton chamber pot has the registration number 258549 and is marked England. A matching ewer and basin would fetch £150–£250. *c.1895; 14in across.* **£25–£30**

Bedroom and toilet ceramics are not limited to chamber pots and ewer and basin sets. The lady of the house would need her dressing table equipment and, before the advent of electric light, candlesticks and tapersticks were essential. Inevitably, objects in daily use were most likely to be damaged and, like the barbers' bowls, may now fetch considerable sums if perfect. Today few of these items would be used, they are for decoration only.

△ **DERBY TAPERSTICK** *This piece is decorated in one of the Derby factory's popular Imari-inspired patterns. In perfect condition and complete with the candle snuffer, its value would be greater.*
1810; 3in high.
£150–£200

◁ **TAPERSTICK** *Fine and rare taperstick with some damage. It is, however, still interesting to collectors since it has the Worcester mark and is decorated with the attractive Japanese-type pattern known as "Finger and Thumb". c.1800; 2in high.* **£200–£250;** *In perfect condition* **£800**

△ **BARBERS' BOWLS,** *identified by the moon-shaped gap that fitted the neck of the man being shaved, were imported from the Far East in quantity. The bowl on the right was made c.1710 at Arita in Japan and decorated in underglaze blue, iron-red, green enamel and*
gilding. The other bowl was made in China about 30 years later and decorated in the Japanese Imari palette, which was highly fashionable at the time. Both bowls 12in. **Each £700–£1,000.**

△ **GERMAN DRESSING TABLE SET**
This rather poor-quality porcelain set was made toward the end of the 19th century. The Neo-classical scenes have been transfer printed, as has the gilding. Almost identical pieces are still being made, a fact which is reflected in the low price. 1890s; Tray 12in long. **£200–£300**

◁△ **DRESSING TABLE SET** *Twenty years after the Derby factory was established c.1750, it began to decorate its porcelain in Japanese Imari style. More than 100 years later, this dressing table set was hand painted with similar designs. By that time, the factory had been renamed Royal Crown Derby, after Queen Victoria's visit in 1890. This set includes assorted pots and jars, a tray, candlesticks and a ringstand (left). 1890; Tray 9in long.* **£1,000**

COLLECTOR'S CHECKLIST

CERAMICS PROBABLY HAVE A WIDER appeal than any other works of art, and most households possess at least one or two interesting items. Many delightful pieces can be bought very cheaply indeed: for instance, you can pick up a 200-year-old plate for less than a pound if you do not mind a hairline crack. At the other extreme are incredibly expensive items, such as a Chinese pottery horse made during the Tang Dynasty (618–907) which sold recently for more than £3,000,000.

The relatively small size of pottery and porcelain objects is an additional reason for their popularity: you can keep adding to your collection without too much risk of running out of space. The broad range of materials, styles, factories – and even decorators – involved gives the collector a wide choice of fields in which to specialize.

Ceramics are often colourful, dramatic and of practical use, factors that have attracted interior decorators as well as more traditional collectors. If you find that objects in your chosen field have become "fashionable" and prices have consequently skyrocketed, remember that many categories overlap and it may be possible to increase your collection with pieces from a related field which are more competitively priced. For instance, while large decorative plates and chargers find a ready market, bowls, since they are less easy to display, may be freely available.

There are probably more fakes, forgeries and reproductions of ceramics than of any other type of antique. A fake is a genuine piece that has been altered, a forgery is an attempt to deceive, while a reproduction is an honest re-creation of an earlier object.

Many early deceptions – such as Worcester and Derby pieces with fake Meissen marks – are now accepted and even sought after by collectors.

Problems tend to arise when reproductions are sold as the genuine article, making them forgeries. A prime example of this is the number of Korean copies of Chinese *famille-rose* and Canton porcelain that were imported merely as decorative items but are now appearing at some small auctions and in some antiques shops in the guise of original pieces.

Every so often a particularly clever deception fools the antiques market. The best measure a collector can take when buying a piece is to question the seller closely; thoroughly examine the item; and remember that fakes are most likely to be produced when the value of originals is extremely high.

Restoration of a piece often reduces its value because it creates doubt as to the degree of damage the restoration may hide.

There can be no substitute for experience and for knowing your field when purchasing old ceramics. It is difficult, for instance, for a beginner to tell some pottery from porcelain, but after examining a variety of pieces this becomes easier. So make a point of inspecting and handling as many pieces as possible, and bear in mind the following points.

TIPS FOR BUYERS

1 Before even thinking about buying ceramics there are three essential things to learn: the difference between pottery and porcelain; the difference between hard- and soft-paste porcelain; and the difference between hand-painted and printed wares.

2 When buying a piece of pottery or porcelain, always assume that there is something wrong with it and that the person selling it knows but is not telling.

3 If a small amount of damage is pointed out to you, check the item carefully for further damage.

4 Does the seller answer your questions openly, or is there a hint of evasion? If so, be wary about buying from that source. If an item seems exceptionally cheap, ask yourself whether you have really found a bargain or whether you are being conned.

5 Check that the material, style, coloration, painting, modelling and gilding are all consistent with the period in which the item was supposed to have been made. Satisfy yourself that the piece is up to the aesthetic standard usual for the factory in question. Poor painting and the use of the wrong colours are often signs of a fake.

6 If the item you wish to buy has a mark, is it the one you would expect to find on a piece of this date and is it the correct size and in the right position? Fakes of

the Chelsea red anchor mark, for example, are often too big.

7 Always ask whether a piece has been restored. If the answer is yes, ask the dealer to what extent; if the answer is no or don't know, ask whether you can test it with a pin (which will glide over original glaze and catch on softer restoration work). If the dealer refuses to allow you to do this, take your custom elsewhere.

8 Prices on tickets are often open to negotiation. Do not be afraid to offer a lower amount.

9 Make sure that the seller gives you a full receipt, including date, attribution and condition report.

COLLECTIONS OF INTEREST
British Museum
Museum Street
London WC1B 3DG
Telephone: 0171 636 1555
Burrell Collection
Pollock Country Park
Glasgow G43 1AT
Telephone: 0141 649 7151
Glaisher Collection
Fitzwilliam Museum
Cambridge CB2 1RB
Telephone: 01223 332 900
Victoria & Albert Museum
Cromwell Road, London SW7 2RL
Telephone: 0171 938 8500
Wallace Collection
Manchester Square
London W1M 6BN
Telephone: 0171 935 0687

In addition, many provincial museums have collections of locally made ceramics, and most of the major manufacturers have their own museums and offer tours around their factories.

CLOCKS & WATCHES

CLOCKS & WATCHES

IT IS EXACTLY TWENTY-SIX YEARS SINCE I WALKED into a bric-a-brac shop in Hastings old town and bought my first clock – a French mantel timepiece costing £12. Unfortunately I simply cannot remember why I decided to buy it, since I was not involved in the business and the sum involved was quite substantial when compared with a wage of 35 pence an hour. However, I am certain that I did not get the idea from a book, since nobody would then have bothered to include such a menial clock in a publication.

I still own the clock, not out of sentimentality but simply because it cost far too much at the time, and for the next 10 years would only have been resaleable at a loss. Today I would admit to being rather attached to it, and in the meantime such clocks have become "rare and sought after" to quote a recent article.

It seems that my first purchase, which initially might have been regarded as a mistake, fits perfectly into the scenario of what has happened to the world of antiques and collecting over the last 15 years, and the pattern looks set to continue. A combination of events – increased wealth, inflation, greater awareness of major events in the art and auction world and, indeed, those early programmes on BBC television – have conspired within the period virtually to exhaust the seemingly endless supply of fine antiques.

I use the word "antique" in the sense in which it used to be employed by the organizers of our most prestigious antiques fairs – any object of good quality and in perfect condition that was manufactured before 1830. These objects have not, of course, disappeared; they have, in many instances, just become prohibitively expensive and difficult to find in the market place. The result has been that, in line with the legal definition, the minimum age for an antique is now generally accepted as being 100 years. Today most antiques fairs and specialist auction houses will judge the suitability of an item on its merit, rather than its period.

The purpose of this pocket guide, which notably does not include the word "antique" in the title, is therefore to try to provide a brief historical outline of the types of clocks and watches most frequently seen at the *Antiques Roadshow* recordings, for these are what most people have in their homes. The illustrations are mainly of items that have been brought along to the programme, including those occasional "finds" that turn up every so often, and with a selection of particular rarities from other sources included to illustrate a point.

Having appeared on the Roadshow as a guest for more years than I would care to admit, my lasting impression is of the way in which people's attitudes have changed toward things that are old. Certainly, expert and visitor alike still harbour a flicker of hope that inside every newspaper parcel is a discovery waiting to be made, but in reality people now have more curiosity and interest in knowing the age and origins of their possessions and in the means of conserving them. It would be satisfying to believe that this short guide will be of help in doing this.

Simon Bull

HISTORICAL SURVEY

The first clocks found in large enough quantities to interest the collector are the mid-16th century table clocks made in Augsburg and Nuremberg.

In 1657–58 the Dutchman Christiaan Huygens devised the pendulum, which revolutionized the timekeeping of clocks. The balance hairspring had a similar effect on watches and portable clocks. So by the end of the 1600s the problem of making fairly accurate domestic clocks and watches had been solved.

London became the centre for the best clocks and watches, and this was the period of the great English clockmakers: East, Fromanteel, Graham, Knibb, Quare and Tompion. English movements exported to Holland were housed in locally made cases, while complete clocks were sent to the rest of Europe, to Turkey and even to China.

As maritime trade grew, so did the need for precision timekeeping. In the late 1700s, the quest was pursued in England and France, culminating in the work of the greatest watchmaker ever, Abraham-Louis Breguet.

In the 1800s, the English stuck to producing handmade clocks, while the French made carriage and mantel clocks with standardized movements. After the middle of the century, both were overtaken by mass-produced clocks from Germany and the U.S. and watches from Switzerland.

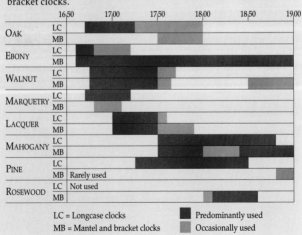

WOODS AND DECORATIONS

Shown here are the periods when particular woods and decorative techniques were most commonly used for English longcase and bracket clocks.

LC = Longcase clocks
MB = Mantel and bracket clocks

Predominantly used
Occasionally used

SHAPES OF CLOCKS

1 BRONZE WALL CLOCK

2 TAVERN CLOCK

3 LONGCASE CLOCK

4 CARRIAGE CLOCK

5 LANTERN CLOCK

6 STATION DIAL CLOCK

7 SKELETON CLOCK

Clocks came in a variety of shapes to suit their intended location and their function.
1 Grand bronze wall clock that may have decorated an 18th-C French interior; also popular in the 19th C. **2** 18th-C tavern, or Act of Parliament, clock.
3 English longcase clock of imposing 18th-C design.

4 Classic French carriage clock, of the type made from *c.*1850.
5 Lantern clock, the first English household clock, made from *c.*1620. **6** Dial clock of the type found on railway stations from *c.*1850. **7** Elegant and complicated French skeleton clock of the Empire period; early 19th C.

How Clocks Work

By the mid-1500s, small table clocks were being made with the movement held between two plates, cut to the same shape and size as the case, and with the dial on top. In the mid-1600s, this construction was adapted to a vertical format for the movements of bracket and longcase clocks. Since then, most clock movements have been of the plated type.

The same is true of watches, except that, in the 1760s, the Frenchman J.A. Lepine invented a system of thin metal braces for each wheel in the train, which allowed much slimmer watches to be made.

The functions of a clock or watch – striking the hours, for instance – are controlled by various "trains", which are incorporated within the movement. A train is a series of gear wheels and pinions running

THE MOTIVE POWER OF CLOCKS

The first type of escapement was the **verge escapement**, known also as a crown-wheel escapement because the teeth were cut to look like a crown.

In the **anchor escapement**, developed c.1670, the pallets resemble a ship's anchor. First used for longcase, tavern and

lantern clocks with a second-beating long pendulum, c.1800 it was used in bracket clocks with a shorter pendulum. English spring-driven bracket clocks were usually fitted with a fusee attached by a cord or chain to the spring barrel.

These two types of escapement were followed by many others.

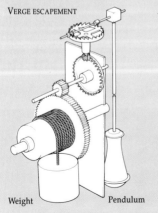

VERGE ESCAPEMENT

Weight   Pendulum

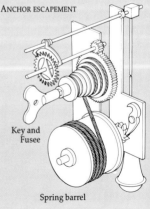

ANCHOR ESCAPEMENT

Key and Fusee

Spring barrel

from the source of power to the function performed; there is normally one train for each function.

Most clocks were driven by weights or coiled springs before the advent of electricity. As it falls, a weight accelerates, and as it unwinds, a spring weakens; so a device, known as an escapement, was needed to allow only some of the driving power to escape at a time. With each swing of the balance, or pendulum, the hands move on slightly as the escapement is briefly unlocked and locked again.

Some spring-driven movements incorporate a fusee to compensate for the weakening of the spring as it unwinds. The fusee is a concave-sided cone cut with a spiral groove. When fully wound, the spring pulls against the narrow end of the fusee; as it unwinds, it works its way toward the wider end.

The Germans used the fusee in the trains for table clocks; by 1700 the French had dispensed with it, but the English used it until the early 1900s, and it is a hallmark of the high quality of English clocks.

The **brocot escapement**, found in French clocks in the 1800s, was usually visible on the dial. The **lever escapement**, developed in 1759 by Thomas Mudge, is still used in mechanical wrist watches. The **cylinder escapement**, perfected by George Graham, and the **dead-beat escapement**, which he invented in 1715, were used respectively for lower priced pocket watches, and for regulators and astronomical clocks.

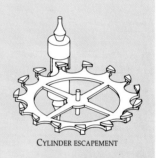

CYLINDER ESCAPEMENT

LEVER ESCAPEMENT

BROCOT ESCAPEMENT   DEAD-BEAT ESCAPEMENT

CLOCK FACES

The dials of English and French clocks were markedly different. While the English kept to a basically rectangular shape, French dials were, from c.1715, circular. Enamelling techniques were more advanced in France, and one-piece enamel dials were produced c.1715–20 for watches and c.1725–35 for clocks. Before this, enamel hour plaques in a cast ormolu frame were used – a style that was revived c.1850.

Enamelled dials were rare in England; watches had them only after the 1740s, and clocks after the 1850s. English dials had an applied chapter ring and spandrels fixed to the dial plate; even after the 1760s a flat brass dial, engraved and silvered, was more usual than enamel. By c.1780, "white" dials, painted and decorated with polychrome spandrels and arches, were common on longcase clocks.

CLOCK DIAL TYPES

The design of a dial and the materials used can reveal when and where it was made and for what type of clock. **1** Silvered and gilt brass dial for a single-hand clock, 18th C. **2** Dial with cast scrollwork panel and dark blue numerals on white enamel plaques, 18th C, revived 19th C. **3** German painted dial with brass centre, late 19th C. **4** Victorian enamel dial with 18th-C design.

3 PAINTED DIAL

1 ENGLISH BRASS DIAL

4 ENAMELLED DIAL

2 FRENCH CAST DIAL

THE FACE

A classic early 18th-century longcase clock face illustrates many of the common elements of all clock faces.
1 Second ring uppermost.
2 Chapter ring with numerals in black. **3** Spandrels of cast and chased brass. **4** Long minute hand and ornate hour hand. **5** One of two apertures for winding keys. **6** Maker's signature. **7** Date aperture.

CLOCK HANDS

Early hands were handmade for each clock; in 1690–1740 ornate hands were still carved, but after 1760 hands were often stamped out. Later, the hands were plainer and closer in size.

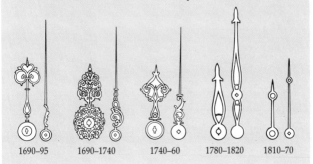

1690–95   1690–1740   1740–60   1780–1820   1810–70

Dials were usually positioned on clock fronts, although on table clocks *c.*1550–1650 they were mostly on top. Touch-pieces by the hour numerals and sturdy single hands allowed the time to be "felt" with the fingertips at night. Clock dials with a single hand were fairly standard before the invention of the pendulum in the 1650s and, by *c.*1675, the balance hairspring for watches. Accuracy was thus refined from 30 minutes a day to within three minutes a week.

Minute hands came into general use as a result of these improvements in timekeeping. Second hands, rarely found on bracket or mantel clocks, were adopted on longcase clocks in the 1670s, along with the anchor escapement and second-beating long pendulum. Second hands, however, were not common on pockets watches before 1800.

Calendar hands for the day of the week, date and so on, which had become common on German tabernacle clocks in the 17th century, again became fashionable in the late 1700s and have remained so. Indeed, there was a late flowering in English precision watches at the end of the 1800s, when many pieces were produced with moon phase and calendar indicators and, often, minute or quarter-repeating mechanisms.

SPANDRELS

These ornate corner pieces, used to embellish clock faces and known as spandrels, were made by brass finishers, who cast the pieces in quantity, finished them by hand and fire-gilded them. Spandrels are a useful aid to dating, since patterns were standardized; all the clocks by particlar makers at particular periods bore the same spandrels.

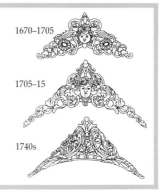

1670–1705

1705–15

1740s

KEYS

Clock keys vary in shape and design, depending on the function they perform and the style of the clock for which they are intended.
1 Typical "crank" key used for winding a longcase clock.
2 and **3** Small double-ended keys, typical of those made for French carriage clocks.
4 Standard brass heart-shaped key for bracket and table clocks used from 1780 to 1900; this design is peculiarly English.
5 and **6** Standard brass keys for English bracket clocks.

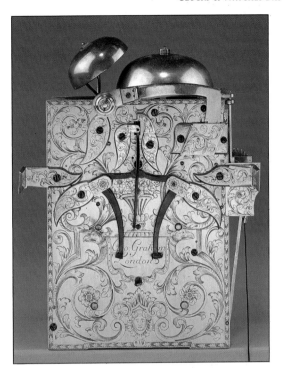

△ **AN ENGRAVED BACKPLATE,** *from clock no. 619 by George Graham, London, c.1725. The engraving on the backplates is a chief glory of English bracket clocks. A plain signature gave way by c.1680 to motifs of scrolling foliage and* *tulips, and, from c.1690, grotesque ornament and birds. Baroque scrolls, common from 1710, became lighter and more Rococo by c.1750. By 1800 engraving took the form of repeated motifs on the edge of the plate; by 1840 only a signature remained.*

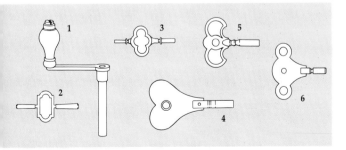

BRACKET &
MANTEL CLOCKS

There is often confusion about the
terms "bracket" and "mantel" clock, but
both are, in effect, table clocks which were
made to sit on top of pieces of furniture,
on shelves or, after the mid-18th century,
on mantelpieces. Contrary to what the
name implies, bracket clocks only rarely
stood on wall brackets. Both these
clocks are among the most collectable of
timepieces, since over the centuries
thousands of them have been made and
wide range of different types exists.
Except for pieces by the top makers,
the price of a good-quality English bracket
clock by a provincial maker can be fairly
reasonable. The same is true of French
mantel clocks, where the variety is
much greater, with cases in the Rococo
period decorated with gilding, marquetry
or ormolu and figures in brass or porcelain;
sometimes entire cases were made from
porcelain in fanciful shapes, such as
elephants or bowers festooned with
flowers and rustic figures.

BRACKET CLOCKS

The introduction of the pendulum into England in 1659 led directly to the development not only of longcase but also of bracket clocks. These wooden-cased clocks derived their name from the wall bracket with which some were provided, but most stood on pieces of furniture and initially were known simply as spring clocks.

Originally most 18th-century examples had a verge escapement; in the 1800s, this was often converted to an anchor escapement, with a heavier, slower pendulum. Movements were framed in vertical plates, and clocks usually ran for eight days.

Similar numbers of cases were made from ebony and ebonized woods as from walnut and, after 1750, mahogany. Very few marquetry cases were made, but some lacquered or japanned bracket clocks were produced in the 18th century.

△ **ARCHITECTURAL–STYLE CLOCK** *made by Samuel Betts a few years after the pendulum's invention. The style, with entablature and pediment, and the dial, with a narrow chapter ring set against an engraved dial plate, are typical of the earliest type of bracket clock.* c.1665; 19in high. **£20,000+**

◁ **GEORGE II CLOCK** *on its original bracket. It is signed for George Graham but was probably made by his pupil, Thomas Mudge, shortly before Graham's death. The "skin" of the bracket slides forward to show a well for storing the winding key.* c.1750; 21in high. **£30,000+**

STYLES OF BRACKET CLOCK

The architectural-style case was superseded *c.*1675 by a plinth-shaped box topped by a dome of changing shape. At first it was cushion moulded (the caddy, or basket top); a concave curved section was added *c.*1720 (the inverted bell top); by 1760 the curves were reversed (the bell top); break-arch cases appeared in the late 1700s, followed by balloon tops; lancet and chamfer tops were in vogue from Regency times.

CADDY, OR BASKET,
TOP, 1670–1725

REPOUSSÉ BASKET
TOP, 1690–1725

INVERTED BELL TOP,
1720–70

BELL TOP,
1760–1810

BREAK-ARCH TOP,
1750–1830

BALLOON TOP,
1780–1820

LANCET TOP,
1810–60

CHAMFER TOP,
1815–40

In the early 1700s, despite the name, most bracket clocks were carried around the house and so had a handle on top of the case; this was, in the main, retained when clocks became more common. Some, such as the Tompion clock below, anticipating the carriage clocks of the 1800s, even had their own travelling cases.

▽ **EBONIZED BRACKET CLOCK** *by Samuel Norton, London, with the original, highly decorated case and dial. The movement was replaced c.1880, when gong striking was added.* Case 1760; 21in high. **£1,000**

△ **EBONY AND SILVER CLOCK** *This exquisite small clock with ornate silver mounts, numbered 460, was made by Thomas Tompion and Edward Banger, reputedly for Queen Anne. It survives with its original oak travelling case. It is unique. 1705; 9in high.* **£400,000**

CHIMING BRACKET CLOC

Although it was made in Germany this chiming bracket clock, in a mahogany case with gilt-metal mounts, reflects 19th-century interest in the classic English taste of 100 years earlier.

The value of clocks made during this revivalist period is determined by both the quality and richness of the case and the sophistication of the strike mechanism. Late 1800s; 21in high. **£2,000**

English bracket clocks were made mainly in London and a few other centres; many of those signed for country makers were simply retailed in the provinces.

▷ **MAHOGANY BREAK-ARCH CLOCK** *signed "Vulliamy". Enamel dials first appeared in England in the 1760s. The face of this clock, with a "triple-pad" arched top, has three enamel discs: one for the main chapter ring and subsidiaries in the arch for setting to strike/silent and for regulating the pendulum. c.1780; 20in high.* **£10,000**

MANTEL CLOCKS

The invention of the spring balance and the pendulum in the 17th century led directly to the evolution of longcase and bracket clocks. Mantel clocks are related to bracket clocks but are generally smaller and shallower and have no carrying handles. They first appeared in France in the 1750s and in Britain a decade later. Before these dates, mantelpieces were not made with shelves capable of taking a clock.

◁ **FRENCH LOUIS XVI MANTEL CLOCK** *signed "Piolaine à Paris", with figures and mounts of gilt brass. Unusually, the case is made of white porcelain; brass or marble was more common. The bezel of the glass covering for the dial is missing. 1780; 14in high.* **£4,000**

▷ **ORMOLU AND BRONZE CLOCK** *by Julien Le Roy of Paris, who was Louis XV's clockmaker. The solid, uncluttered design of the case is typical of the transitional period between Louis XV and Louis XVI. 1775; 11in high.* **£4,000**

ORMOLU CLOCK STYLES

The word "ormolu" comes from the French and describes the gilt finish on bronze or brass. French clocks, furniture mounts and many 18th- and 19th-century objets d'art are described as "ormolu-mounted". The process, which used highly toxic mercury, was superseded by electroplating.

EGYPTIAN STYLE, LATE 18TH CENTURY

ROCOCO STYLE, MID-18TH CENTURY

Shapes and forms of decoration were at their most varied during the 18th century in France. Talented craftsmen and designers were attracted to the courts of both Louis XIV and Louis XV, when highly ornate Rococo clocks were made in combinations of porcelain, ormolu, bronze, marble and *vernis martin* – a form of lacquer.

The best makers continued to serve under Louis XVI as well as during the Revolutionary and Empire period, when design followed the Neo-classical style.

▷ **RARE FRENCH PORTICO CLOCK**
with gridiron pendulum. The base and columns are of ribbed blue glass with ormolu mounts, a style referred to as "Palais Royal" after the area of Paris where these clocks were sold. 1840; 24in high. **£5,000+**

FAMOUS CLOCKMAKERS

The makers' names (below, with dates of working) appear most often on standard Paris-made movements.

H. MARC (1820–60); LE ROY ET FILS (1830–90); A. BROCOT (1840–65); V.A.P. (1840 onward); VINCENTI ET CIE (1850–70); C.A. RICHARD ET CIE (1850–1900); JAPY FRÈRES (1850 onward); MARTI ET CIE (1860–1900); DUVERDREY ET BLONQUEL (1870 onward); S. MARTI (1900 onward).

LOUIS XV ORMOLU AND MARBLE, 18TH CENTURY

LOUIS XV STYLE, 19TH CENTURY

EMPIRE STYLE, 19TH CENTURY

The 19th century saw an even greater production of mantel clocks, since the Industrial Revolution led to the rise of a large and prosperous middle class and an increased demand for luxury items. This was coupled with technical advances in the skills needed to produce such clocks. The styles of the 18th century were revived, but were modified to reduce production costs and suit the smaller rooms of the average home. Victorian copies are, therefore, generally smaller than the originals of the previous century, and sometimes lack the artistic flair and clarity of design.

Most French mantel clocks found in Britain today are unlikely to be genuine 18th-century pieces, since Victorian copies abound. However, 19th-century movements are much more reliable than those of the previous century.

▽ **ORMOLU AND MARBLE STRIKING CLOCK** *in Louis XIV style, with an enamel face. The quality of the mountings compares favourably with 18th-century pieces. Mid-19th century; 12in high.* **£1,000**

▽ **GILT BRASS MANTEL CLOCK**
The style of the case is a Victorian hybrid incorporating elements from the reigns of both Louis XV and XVI. The elaborate scrolls, flowers and asymmetrical curves are features of Rococo decoration. The dial, known as a cartouche dial, was popular in France from 1685 to 1750 and was revived in the 19th century. 1875; 15in high. **£600–£800**

◁ **FRENCH ORMOLU
MANTEL CLOCK** *housing
a two-train movement
made by Japy Frères and
with the original glass
dome intact. Japy Frères
produced a great many
movements, which were
installed in various grades
of cases. The cherubs on
the case of this example
are of excellent quality.
1875; 20in high.*
£800–£1,000

VICTORIAN BRONZE CLOCKS

During the 19th century
casting techniques were
developed that enabled the
production in great numbers
of high-quality bronzes. As
a result, some of the most
impressive Victorian clock
cases are composed of
sculpted bronze figures,
animals or objects, with
the clock movement an
integral part of the
design. Favourite
subjects

included figures from popular
literary works and from the
mythology of ancient Greece
and Rome.

◁ **BRONZE AND MARBLE
MANTEL CLOCK** *with a
white enamel dial
signed "Marshall,
Paris". The figure
suggests "Learning"
or "Philosophy".
1870; 18in
high.* **£600**

In comparison with highly ornate French clocks, English mantel clocks usually had wooden cases, with decoration used sparingly. The finest examples, however, were superb quality, usually non-striking, timepieces for the library, study or boudoir.

△ **LARGE MAHOGANY CLOCK,** *probably intended for a large hall. The German movement is of good quality, with a series of sonorous strikes. 1900; 32in high.* **£300**

Wooden mantel clocks found great favour in the late 19th century, when elegant furniture in the style of Sheraton was being revived. The cases, mostly made from mahogany and oak, were fashioned in a diverse range of shapes. Decoration often took the form of boxwood stringing on the edges, or panels of imported marquetry ovals, quadrants, shells and other motifs.

The cases were English made, but many of the movements were imported from Europe.

▽ **MUSICAL MANTEL CLOCK**
A British-made clock, cased in oak, with a musical movement made by the Symphonium company. A selection of different discs was available. 1900; 10in high. **£400**

◁ **OAK MANTEL CLOCK** *by the Glasgow maker James Muirhead, who worked between 1817 and 1841. Indications of quality are the plain carving and the existence of a fusee within the movement. 1840; 9½in high.* **£800**

THE MANTEL SET

By the 1830s the practice
of flanking a mantel clock
with paired ornaments on
a mantelpiece led to the
garniture de cheminée, a
mantel set consisting of a clock
and matching sidepieces, often
candelabra, which enjoyed a
vogue in the 19th century.

▽△ **FRENCH MANTEL SET** of
*veined marble and gilt brass
with a symbolic eagle on the
clock (top). The movement
(below) has a "feather" spring,
invented by A. Brocot c.1830.
1880; Clock 21in high.* **£2,000**

▽ *The pendulum is in a
"spagnolette" (or sunburst)
shape, one of the most popular
18th-century French designs.*

LONGCASE CLOCKS

For many people longcase clocks, or grandfather clocks as they are rather affectionately known, conjure up romantic images of the past. They remain some of the most popular, and expensive, timepieces ever made. As pieces of furniture with a timekeeping function, their cases were often made by skilled cabinet makers and tended to follow the decorative style of the day. The most valuable, and often the rarest, longcase clocks are those that were made in London between 1660 and 1720 – the best period for English clocks. It was the era of clockmakers such as Thomas Tompion, Daniel Quare, Joseph Knibb and George Graham, whose best clocks, both longcase and bracket, fetch hundreds of thousands of pounds at auction. There are, however, many highly respected London-based and provincial clockmakers whose pieces are more reasonably priced. Longcase clocks always cost a significant amount of money, but can be an excellent investment.

Longcase Clocks

The introduction of the long pendulum in the Netherlands in the late 1650s soon led to the development of longcase clocks. These attractive floor-standing pieces, designed with long trunks to protect the weights and pendulum, were first produced in England – where they became known as grandfather clocks. Although they were most popular in England and in America, where they are called tallcase clocks, longcase clocks were produced in small numbers all over Europe.

Early longcase clocks used verge escapements and fairly short pendulums. It was only with the development of the more accurate anchor escapement in the 1670s that longer pendulums were made to beat the seconds.

Since only the wealthy could afford early examples, they were made with expensive woods such as ebony or mahogany, or finished with ornate decoration such as walnut marquetry.

Although the decoration and finish vary, all longcase clocks share certain components.

Hood — Pediment

Seat board — Fret for sound to escape

Lock — Trunk

Lenticle to view the pendulum — Trunk door

Base —

Foot

△ **Burr walnut longcase clock**
The date of this clock is indicated by both the arched dial (post c.1720) and the flat-topped trunk door (pre c.1730). It was made by William Webster, a pupil of Thomas Tompion, and has an ogee moulded top with ball-and-spire finials. The arched dial includes a subsidiary strike/silent ring; the hands are pierced blue steel. 8ft 4in high. **£5,000–£7,000**

◁▽△ **PARQUETRY-INLAID CLOCK**
Both the engraving around the date
aperture and the spandrels on the
face of this walnut clock, signed by
Sam Barrow of London, are typical
of clocks made at this time. Although
the parquetry (geometric) inlay
dates from the 1800s, good-quality
work like this does not affect the
value. However, the unsympathetic
replacement of the base plinth does.
1700; 6ft 8in high. **£5,000**

The period 1670 to 1720 was the heyday of the English longcase clock. It was also the time of some of the greatest ever clockmakers, including Daniel Quare, Thomas Tompion, Joseph Knibb and George Graham.

In the early 1700s, longcase clocks became increasingly tall. Before about 1710 it was usual to push up the top of the clock to gain access to the winding holes, but after this date it became necessary to make a door in the hood. This extra height meant that dials, which include the chapter ring and spandrels, also grew – a good method of dating clocks.

Most London-made longcase clocks have an eight-day movement, although some were made to run for a month, three months or even longer after winding.

▷ QUEEN ANNE LONGCASE CLOCK
Japanned in ivory, the rarest and most desirable colour, this clock was made by Daniel Quare (1647–1724), one of England's finest clockmakers. Introduced in the early 1700s, japanning is a type of imitation lacquer which became a fashionable finish for longcase clocks between 1720 and 1790. Unfortunately, the hood of this piece lacks its finials. c.1710; 8ft 1in high. **£220,000**

DATING DIALS

The simplest method of dating an English longcase clock is by examining the dial for size and for the presence of certain features. Before 1690 dials measured 10 inches or less. Dials of 11 inches were then used until 1715, when 12 inches became standard.

1660–65
8-INCH DIAL,
SMALL NUMERALS

1665–90
10-INCH DIAL,
DATE APERTURE ADDED

◁△ **MARQUETRY LONGCASE CLOCK**
*The concave mouldings below the
hood of this walnut and marquetry
clock confirm that it dates from
the early 1700s. Convex moulding
would indicate the latter part of
the 17th century. The trunk door
opens to reveal the pendulum and
weights. It was made by Eliot of
London. c.1715.* **£26,500**

1685–95	1695–1720	1720	1720
11-INCH DIAL,	12-INCH DIAL,	12-INCH DIAL,	12-INCH DIAL,
:ONDS RING ADDED	LARGER MINUTE RING	FIRST ARCHED DIAL	ARCHED MOON DIAL

As the 18th century progressed, the expanding and increasingly prosperous middle classes were able to afford longcase clocks, and their popularity increased. They were articles of prestige not restricted to the nobility.

Many of the pieces made at this time were produced by provincial makers as the manufacture of longcase clocks moved away from the main cities. The cases followed the styles of city-made clocks, although they were sometimes as much as 20 years behind the times.

City-made movements, from centres such as Birmingham, were put inside locally produced cases, usually of oak or pine. This was then painted to simulate an exotic wood, such as mahogany.

△ **CHINOISERIE LONGCASE CLOCK**
On the door of this clock, the Chinese-style japanned decoration is raised to imitate lacquer. That on the plinth and sides is, by contrast, both simpler and applied on a flat surface. The clock lacks its finials. c.1740; 7ft 11in high. **£10,000**

△ **GEORGE III MAHOGANY LONGCASE CLOCK,** *made in London by Conyers Dunlop, with a small dial at the top of the face which can be set to "strike" or "silent". The wood of the door shows extremely fine "flame"-patterned grain. 1770; 7ft high.* **£3,000**

Clock Case Styles

The designs of clock cases reflect the general trend, in cabinet-making terms, of style, details and finishes in the periods in which the clocks were produced.

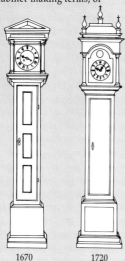

1670   1720   1730   1770

Types of Finial

Finials were of wood or metal, gilded and lacquered, usually in a simple urn or orb design; later an eagle was often used.

The elaborate finials below, on a Dutch clock from 1740, show the Angel Gabriel, Father Time and Atlas supporting the world.

PAINTED DIALS

Although long considered inferior to clocks with brass dials, those with painted dials are now sought after. Painted and lightly fired, these "white" dials were first advertised in the early 1770s. By the 1780s they had become popular and remained so, on provincial longcases, until the 1840s.

△▽▷ **TWO PAINTED DIALS**
The battle scene (above) and figures representing the seasons come from the Scottish clock (right). Its origin is indicated by the spiral columns and cross-banding decoration. Other common themes for painted dials, besides battle scenes, are fruit or flowers, as shown on this West Country example (below).

▽ PROVINCIAL LONGCASE CLOCK
The canted corners of the plinth and verre églomisé (glass with gilded decoration) below the swan-neck pediment are typical of Lancashire longcases made in this period. The columns on the hood and trunk are another common feature. It was made by Joseph Finney of Liverpool. 1780s; 7ft 8in high. **£4,500–£6,000**

△ PAINTED LONGCASE CLOCK
Pine cases, with painted decoration, are common on north European longcase clocks as is the arched hood. The mouldings on this mid-18th century example have been picked out in gold leaf. 1750s; 8ft high. **£2,500**

After 1800 few longcase clocks were made in cities; production had almost entirely moved to the provinces where demand was higher. London clockmakers did, however, continue to make regulator-type longcase clocks.

During the Victorian period it became fashionable to decorate the plain cases of longcase clocks with carving. Where this embellishment is of a high standard, like that found on clocks that were carved in the

△ **OAK CLOCK** *signed by George Maynard of Lavenham. When it was made, in the late 1700s, this clock had a plain case, finials and a 30-hour movement. In Victorian times, the case was carved, the finials lost and an 8-day movement installed. 6ft 6in high.* **£900**

△ **CARVED LONGCASE CLOCK**
The Victorians were very keen to "improve" the plain cases of earlier clocks. Sometimes this made a piece more decorative and enhanced its value (left), but the carving on this clock case is too crude. Late 18th century; 8ft 2in high. **£750**

17th and 18th centuries, this may increase the value of a piece.

By the late 1800s, the fashion for longcase clocks had ended. Other clocks were cheap, easy to use and more in keeping with the smaller homes of the times.

△ **FRENCH EMPIRE LONGCASE CLOCK** *Originally a plain early 1800s clock, its case was later decorated with fine marquetry and ormolu mounts. The dial came from an earlier clock by Lepine, who had been active in the 1700s. 1820–40; 6ft 8in high.* **£4,000–£6,000**

LONGCASE REGULATOR

Regulators are precision clocks against which others could be set. Many were made in Vienna, including this example, although they were also produced in London. This piece has a rectilinear case and silvered dial. It also has a rather unusual three-train *grande sonnerie* movement. 1815–30; 6ft 2in high. **£10,000+**

Travelling Clocks

The carriage clock dates from the late
18th century. At that time, families would
only have had a couple of clocks in the
home and these would have been carried
around the house to where they were
needed. Since the carriage clock was small
and light it proved ideal for such use.
Although the clocks were not made
primarily for use in carriages,
when people travelled they generally took
a carriage clock along. Initially all such
clocks were sold with a travelling case, but
over the years most cases have been lost.
The variety of carriage clocks is enormous,
with values varying according to the
complication of the striking mechanism,
the decoration of the case, and whether the
clock has calendar dials or a complicated
escapement. The marine chronometer was
another form of clock designed for portable
use. It was a highly accurate timepiece
which was developed in the 18th century
to determine a ship's east–west
position, or longitude, at sea.

TRAVELLING CLOCKS

The development of spring-driven mechanisms in the early 16th century enabled the manufacture of small timepieces. At first they took the form of large watches, between three and five inches in diameter, known as "tambour" watches. Accuracy was improved in the 1670s with the invention of the balance hairspring.

Travelling, or carriage, clocks were adapted from rectangular portable clocks, but had the balance and escapement at the top of the movement, rather than on the backplate. They were usually made of brass, with glazed sides and top and a carrying handle.

The first carriage clock was made by Abraham-Louis Breguet for Napoleon I – then on his Egyptian Campaign of 1798 – who insisted that all his generals should have one.

◁ **FRENCH OVAL CARRIAGE CLOCK** *with an enamel dial, made by A. Dumas and complete with its original leather travelling case. It is half-size, which adds to the appeal for a collector, since miniature clocks are generally more valuable than standard-size clocks of an equivalent quality. 1870; 4in high.* **£400**

CARRIAGE CLOCK STYLES

Different sizes and styles were used for carriage clock cases, which had various degrees of elaboration. Cases might be embellished with engraving or set with porcelain or enamelled panels instead of plain side glasses. English carriage clocks are in general superior to French ones.

CORNICHE

GORGE

EMPIRE

▷ **A STANDARD AND A MINIATURE CARRIAGE CLOCK** *The piece on the left has elegant Breguet hands and the original leather travelling case.*

The miniature clock was made in France but retailed by a jeweller in Darlington, County Durham, although the name is no longer legible.
Standard clock *1885; 6in high.* **£150**
Miniature clock *1890; 3in high.* **£200**

◁ **FRENCH COMBINATION CLOCK** *Unusually, this clock is combined with an aneroid barometer and is complete with its original travelling case. On the top, inset above the barometer, is a magnetic compass. There is also a central thermometer. 1880; 7in high.* **£1,100**

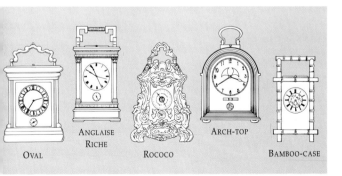

OVAL   ANGLAISE RICHE   ROCOCO   ARCH-TOP   BAMBOO-CASE

The demand for travelling clocks finally took off in the second half of the 19th century, when the coming of the railways revolutionized travel. The greatest numbers were made between 1880 and 1900. After World War I, however, the production of fine-quality carriage clocks went into decline.

The small scale of carriage clocks makes them well suited to the modern home, and good-quality unadulterated pieces can be extremely costly.

△ **ENGLISH CARRIAGE CLOCK** *with a case made of rosewood and a double fusee movement typical of such clocks. The case has been repolished and the dial repainted, which in this case affects the value adversely. Many clocks with an English retailer's name are, in fact, French. Genuine English clocks, however, can usually be distinguished by their use of a fusee and chain. 1850; 9in high.* **£1,000–£1,3000**

STRIKING MECHANISMS

The most basic type of clock was non-striking. Others had various striking sequences: hour and half-hour; quarter-hour; and *petite sonnerie* (quarter-striking with a strike/silent lever). Clocks with a *grande sonnerie* mechanism had a three-position lever that could be set to strike the hour and quarter at each quarter; to strike only at the hour; or to silence the strike completely.

△ **GILT BRASS CLOCK** *with a* grande sonnerie *striking mechanism and porcelain panels to the front and sides. Decorative panels were added to carriage clocks from about 1870. 1905; 7in high.* **£3,500**

◁ **FULL-CALENDAR CLOCK** *This French piece has three subsidiary dials (day of week, month and date) and an early original lever platform. It is signed "Dent à Paris". Dent was an English retailer whose clocks were made in Paris. The cast case is ornate for the period. 1860; 6in high.* **£1,200–£1,500**

▷ **LATE FRENCH CARRIAGE CLOCK** *housed in an "Anglaise"-style case, presumably intended for the English market. Multicoloured* champlevé *enamel is, unusually, combined with Italian micromosaic panels on the side and rear door. 1887; 7in high.* **£4,000–£6,000**

◁ **MINIATURE FRENCH CARRIAGE CLOCK** *with a case made of ivory. The dial and hands are well preserved, but the case is cracked in several places and the replacement brass handle in the shape of a semicircle is not in keeping with the whole. The movement is unsigned. Late 19th century; 2½in high.* **£300–£400**

NOVELTY
CLOCKS

It is impossible to detail all the variations
that have been utilized by clockmakers to
produce novel clocks. Their ingenuity
seems to have known no bounds, and
they delighted in solving complex
problems, only to confound the public with
their skill. Novelty frequently lay in the
form of the case or in automata: as early as
1580 clocks were produced in Germany
in the form of a complete miniature galleon
with moving sailors and firing cannons.
It was from 1800 onward, however,
that the most fanciful creations
proliferated, such as the clock in which a
figure of Cupid on top "sharpens" his
arrow against a rotating grindstone every
hour. But perhaps the most intriguing are
the "mystery" clocks that range from
those in which the movement and
pendulum are so well concealed that it is
difficult for the layman to detect how even
a conventional mechanism works to those,
such as the rolling ball clocks, which appear
to provide their own motive power.

NOVELTY CLOCKS

Made to delight and amuse, novelty clocks have been produced since the 16th century. Novelty may consist in automaton action, an unusual case or the oblique way the time is shown or the clock driven.

Early German clocks were often in the form of animals, calvaries or the Madonna and Child. Many had some form of automaton, such as limbs that moved on the hour or eyes that flicked back and forth in time with the escapement. Picture clocks were also fairly common.

In the 1700s, the French took up the theme of animal clocks and produced fine examples in ormolu and bronze, often with porcelain flowers. Negro clocks, reflecting increased trade with the West Indies and America, were popular in the early 1800s.

By the end of the century, these had been overtaken by "industrial" clocks, resembling pieces of machinery, and skeleton clocks, in which parts of the movement were clearly visible.

◁ **BRONZE MANTEL CLOCK** *This French clock has a silk suspension movement visible through the skeletonized dial. It is set in a lyre-shaped case, flanked by a Classical female figure of very good quality, and stands on a rectangular base with a finely cast panel of putti. c.1820; 23in high.* **£2,000**

▷ **BLACK FOREST PICTURE CLOCK** *A rare, high-quality clock, with an eight-day movement by Sattele Eisenbach. The frame and picture swing away from the dial like a door, and the leopard's eyes move to and fro in time with the swing of the pendulum. c.1860; 12in high.* **£2,000**

◁ **MUSICAL PICTURE CLOCK**
In addition to the clock movement, the frame of this unusual Swiss automaton picture clock contains a musical box, and the lute player moves his head and right hand in time with the music. c.1860; 3ft 1in high. **£2,000**

▷ **WATERFALL CLOCK** *Some of the most entertaining clocks are those in which revolving glass rods simulate water spouting into a basin below. Here, the case is wooden, while the dial and fish's head from which the "water" flows are of gilt brass. 1860; 9in high.* **£700**

◁ **ARCHITECTURAL SKELETON CLOCK** *Clocks with the frame holding the movement reduced to a bare "skeleton" originated in France in the late 1700s, but most of those to be found today were produced in Victorian England; this clock was made in London. 1860; 7½in high.* **£1,500**

Modern reproductions are often seen of an unusual novelty clock: the rolling ball clock developed by William Congreve in 1808. A ball rolls down a zig-zag channel in a tilted tray, which reverses when the ball reaches the end of the groove. This acts as the escapement for a spring-driven movement.

A variation on this type is a clock, first made in America in 1884, featuring a flying escapement which allows a ball on the end of a thread to wind and unwind around two posts set in an otherwise conventional clock.

▷ **LIGHTHOUSE CLOCK**
The revolving head of this French novelty clock, set with a barometer and twin thermometers, is driven by a large spring barrel in the base. Originally the piece was gilded, with silvered highlights such as windows and balustrade. c.1900; 17in high. **£1,200–£1,500**

◁ **THE "FLICK" CLOCK,**
also known as a "ticket" clock, was patented in 1904. It was an early form of digital clock in which cards with the numerals for the hours and minutes are released by the movement of toothed wheels. This example, in a fine brass case, was made in Germany by Junghans. 1905; 5in high.
£250–£300

MYSTERY CLOCKS

Clocks in which there is no obvious link between the dial and the movement that drives the hands, or with a pendulum that appears to swing freely, are known as mystery clocks. They were popular in France, where numerous clocks with glass dials and cases of only fair quality were made. However, many fine makers, including Cartier in the 1920s and 1930s, produced elegant and elaborate mystery clocks.

△ **SWISS MYSTERY CLOCK** *of rock crystal, gold, jade and citrine, with diamond-set hands and hour markers. It was part of a limited edition recently made by Imhof in homage to Cartier's Art Deco clocks. 6in high.* **£15,000**

▽ **FRENCH MYSTERY CLOCK** *cast in spelter, a cheap substitute for bronze. The face and pendulum swing from side to side in an uncanny way, driven by a tiny pendulum hidden behind the dial. c.1900; 12in high.* **£150**

◁ **"LA MYSTÉRIEUSE" CLOCK** *by the Hamburg American Clock Co. A glass disc behind the dial, with its toothed edge concealed by the frame, is driven by the movement in the base and provides the power to move the hands. 1912; 9in high.* **£150**

WALL
CLOCKS

From the first half of the 18th century,
wall-mounted timepieces were a common
fixture in most public buildings, taverns
and inns. An advantage of these wall clocks
was that the large face could be seen
clearly at a distance. In addition, only the
height of the room limits the height at
which the clock can be mounted and, with
no base or plinth in contact with the floor,
wall clocks cannot be knocked by
passers-by. The earliest wall clocks are
lantern clocks, many of which were
converted into mantel or table clocks in the
Victorian period. These clocks are also
widely forged, so collectors should take
extra care before purchasing. Forgery is not
generally a problem with other types of
wall clocks, however. The most collectable
items today are "Vienna regulators",
the pendulum of which was housed in a
case shaped like a miniature longcase clock.
Also highly prized are well-decorated
examples of French cartel clocks, which
were introduced in the 18th century.

WALL CLOCKS

Weight-driven wall clocks with bulky openwork iron frames in the Gothic style were the first domestic timepieces. From *c*.1650, however, many wall clocks were spring driven.

The first English wall clock was the single-handed brass lantern clock topped by a bell. These were made from *c*.1620 until *c*.1720 in London and into the 1800s elsewhere.

At first, English wall clocks resembled the hood of a longcase clock, and had short pendulums and weights that hung below. With the invention of the anchor escapement *c*.1670, protective cases were added.

Spring-driven clocks, such as the drop dial and the common Victorian wall dial, had the movement box hidden behind a glazed round painted dial.

▷ ACT OF PARLIAMENT CLOCK
This early example has a typically prominent signature, William Scafe, at the base of the dial. The case design follows that of longcase clocks. 1725; 5ft 6in high. **£8,000**

WALL CLOCK SHAPES

The earliest wall clocks had long pendulums like those in longcase clocks and were weight driven (usually going for about 30 hours). The first spring-driven wall clocks with short pendulums (running for eight days) date from *c*.1750.

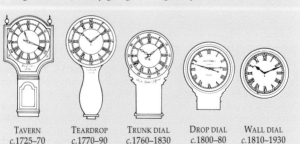

TAVERN	TEARDROP	TRUNK DIAL	DROP DIAL	WALL DIAL
c.1725–70	*c*.1770–90	*c*.1760–1830	*c*.1800–80	*c*.1810–1930

▷ **CARTEL CLOCK** *with a movement made in Switzerland and a French-made case, since the French were better at fashioning ormolu. The case style is early Neo-classical, with a hint of the Rococo evident in the angled female heads. c.1770; 24in high.* **£3,000+**

△ **AMERICAN BANJO CLOCK** *with panels of transfer-printed glass. These clocks were first made in the Federal period (1790–1820) in America, and were revived to celebrate the centenary of the 1776 Declaration of Independence. c.1815; 3ft 4in high.* **£5,000**

△ **WALL REGULATOR** *This Vienna clock, with a walnut case adorned with architectural details, was made in the Germanic Biedermeier period (early 1800s). Such clocks have a single driving weight, which frequently runs for a month. 1830; 34in high.* **£4,500**

The Act of Parliament, or tavern, clock originated in Britain in the 1720s. The name derives from an Act of 1797 taxing all clocks, which meant that many people were forced to rely on clocks in inns and taverns. The tax threatened to put clock-makers out of business, however, and was repealed a year later.

In the mid-1700s, a cottage industry in the Black Forest of Germany made clocks with wooden movements and cases that led to the cuckoo clock. By contrast, Viennese clockmakers in the early 1800s produced precision wall regulators with fine glazed cases and enamel dials. From the early 18th century, French clockmakers made great numbers of cartel clocks, often in ornate cases by leading cabinet makers or *bronziers*. Cartel clocks were revived in the 19th century.

△ "**DROP DIAL**" **WALL CLOCK** *The elaborately inlaid and lacquered decoration incorporates mother-of-pearl inlay. This piece, in good condition, is equally valuable as an item of furniture and as a timepiece. 1860; 24in high.* **£400–£600**

THE LYRE-SHAPED CLOCK

Made from the end of the 18th century, lyre clocks are related in form to American banjo-shaped clocks. They were used both as wall-hanging clocks and, with the addition of an easel back-strut, as boudoir or bedside clocks.

▷ **LYRE-SHAPED CLOCK**
This French wall clock is complete with an enamel face, cast ormolu decoration on a red marble case, and a velour-covered backboard. It has a spring-driven, eight-day mechanism. 1900; 16in high. **£400**

◁ **"DROP DIAL" WALL CLOCK,** so called because of the small trunk below the dial where the pendulum swings. This piece is made of mahogany and has a fusee movement that strikes the hours on a bell. After c.1870, strike on gongs rather than bells became more usual. The original signature of "Thomas of Lincoln" (an English maker) appears on the painted dial. 1870; 16in wide. **£1,250**

▷ **AMERICAN COLONIAL WALL CLOCK** with a mahogany and parcel-gilt case. The painted dial has floral spandrels and is pierced so that the mechanism can be seen. The picture of a colonial public building is typical of this type of good-quality spring-driven clock, which was made for the home market, not for export. c.1870; 24in high. **£400–£600**

◁ **ENGLISH MAHOGANY WALL CLOCK** Unlike most of these classic Victorian clocks, which have fusee pendulum movements, this one has a platform balance escapement. The glass over the dial is held in place by a brass bezel. The face of this good-quality piece is clearly signed "Penney of Cambridge". 1875; 15in wide. **£400**

Mass-Produced Clocks

The first clocks that can in any way be termed mass produced were those made in the early 1800s by the Japy family. These clockmakers worked in France, close to the border with Switzerland, and were, therefore, influenced by Swiss working methods.

In the early 1800s, they began to use machinery for making clock parts and slowly progressed to producing complete, standard-sized movements, which were supplied to the makers of decorative clock cases. Prior to this, all clocks were made largely by hand, and the English continued to produce high-quality handmade clocks until well into the 19th century. From about the mid-1800s, however, clockmaking in both France and England was increasingly threatened by cheap mass-produced clocks from America and Germany. Usually spring-driven shelf clocks in wooden cases, with eight-day mechanisms, they were made in such numbers, to satisfy a growing middle-class market, that bracket and longcase clocks were virtually eclipsed.

MASS-PRODUCED CLOCKS

It was an American, Eli Terry, who first mass produced complete clocks. In 1807, having received an order for 4,000 clocks to be made within three years, he built a factory to make the necessary parts, using water-driven machine tools. Eight years later he built another factory, where he produced large, weight-driven shelf clocks. These were followed in the 1850s by smaller spring-driven models, such as "steeple pattern" and "gingerbread" clocks, and the industry took off.

The first American shelf clocks were shipped to Britain

◁ **MAHOGANY MANTEL CLOCK**
by the Boston maker W.H. Young. This veneered eight-day clock with an arched top and fine carving below the dial is of a type usually referred to as a mantel regulator, after its distinctive pendulum, which could be adjusted by hand. 1850; 19in high. **£800**

▷ **"STEEPLE" OR "GOTHIC" SHELF CLOCK** *A cheaply made version of a popular design, this clock has a stamped dial, the glass door is undecorated, and the veneers on the case are thin. Thousands of such bottom-of-the-market clocks were made and exported worldwide. 1885; 19in high.* **£50**

◁ **"REPEATER" ALARM CLOCK**
Practical looking and robust, this eight-day clock by Seth Thomas is unusual in that it automatically resets for the same time each day. The original instruction label (below) still exists inside the back door. 1890; 9in high. **£100–£200**

in 1842; by the late 1800s, they were sold by the thousand, at very low prices, all over the world. Distinctive features of these clocks include an overall sturdiness of construction, the case shapes – notably Gothic or arched – glazed and often decorated doors and transfer-printed panels below the dial. Makers' names are usually marked on the dial, and some cases contain trade or instruction labels.

△ **SHELF CLOCK** by the Ansonia Clock Co., Connecticut, veneered in local spruce wood which has been stained and polished to look like more expensive mahogany. The print on the door below the dial is probably a replacement, since it does not entirely cover the glass. 1885; 12in high. **£50**

▷ **SHELF CLOCK** by the New Haven Clock Co. of the type known as a "gingerbread" clock. The name derived from the raised pattern, which was produced by steaming the wood then pressing it into a mould in much the same way that gingerbread was traditionally made. 1900; 22in high. **£125**

The main rivals to American mass-produced clocks were those made in the Black Forest area of Germany. Clockmaking began there in the 1600s; by the 1720s it had become a regular cottage industry, and the following 100 years are considered the region's most notable period for handmade wooden clocks.

But competition from the U.S. in the 1850s meant that small workshops declined and big factories were set up. Bracket and mantel clocks were not made in any quantity until the 1870s, when it became possible to mass produce springs, but by the 1890s eight million clocks were being turned out a year.

Most surviving Black Forest clocks date from the 1870s to the 1930s. If unsigned, it can be hard to tell them from American ones, but German cases are stained, not veneered, and a brass hook and pin secure the door.

▷ **FAKE MARBLE MANTEL CLOCK**
In the late 1800s, slate and marble clocks were particularly popular in Britain. To satisfy demand at the cheaper end of the market, the Hamburg American Clock Co. produced wooden-case clocks lacquered and painted, as here, to give the effect of marble. 1890; 12in high. **£80**

◁ **FRUITWOOD MANTEL CLOCK**
Although the clock's architectural style is conventional, with finials and carved roof-tile decoration, its mechanism is unusual: the alarm activates a music box (above) containing several cylinders which play different tunes. 1895; 10in high. **£150**

◁ **"FOUR GLASS" CLOCK** so called because all four sides are glass. The design was popularized in France, but lower-quality copies were soon being made by Black Forest makers. Although the clock appears to be made of brass, it is probably a mixture of brass and spelter; the lion and the base were both cast in spelter, then gilded. 1895; 16in high. **£150**

▷ **ALARM CLOCK** of "steeple-pattern" type. The adjustable "grid-iron" pendulum is marked "R=A", for "Retard/Advance"; when a tiny nut below this dial is turned toward the R, the clock runs more slowly and vice versa. 1900; 17in high. **£50**

◁ **THIRTY-HOUR STRIKING CLOCK** in an Art Deco-type oak case, with gilt, stamped floral spandrels in 18th-century style in the corners of the face. It is typical of Black Forest clocks exported to Britain, particularly those made by the Hamburg American Clock Co., whose trademark of crossed arrows appears behind the pendulum. 1920; 12in high. **£50**

WATCHES

Over the last three centuries,
watches have developed from large,
rather inaccurate objects to slim, elegant
pieces with split-second timing.
Early pocket watches, dating from the
17th and 18th centuries, are highly
sought after and can command tens of
thousands of pounds at auction.
The market for women's watches is
developing quickly, especially for cocktail
watches from the 1930s. The passion for
collecting wrist watches is a relatively
recent phenomenon.
It started in the 1980s as a reaction
to the ubiquity and cheapness of quartz
movement watches. The vogue for
stylish and mechanically complicated
pieces, from both before and after World
War II, has led some makers to put their
most popular models back into
production. While the manufacture of the
Rolex Oyster never stopped, that of the
Jaeger Le Coultre Reverso has been
revived. The most desirable wrist
watches are generally those with both
a high degree of mechanical
sophistication and a good maker.

POCKET WATCHES

The development of the steel mainspring in the early 1500s allowed smaller clock mechanisms to be made. This led to the introduction of portable timepieces and, later, watches.

The first pocket watches, made in the late 1500s, were fairly large. Over the next century, they became smaller and more elaborately decorated, and metal dials gave way to enamel.

Early cases were covered in leather, held in place with pins; later a shagreen cover was common. The decoration of cases has been diverse, including plain, engraved and embossed metal as well as enamel work.

Although invented in the 1760s, the lever escapement was not used until the 1830s. Within 20 years, it had supplanted all other movements.

△ **EARLY ENGLISH WATCH** *This fine watch, with a verge escapement, has a silver case covered in leather and decorated with silver pinwork. The dial includes a calendar ring and blued-steel calendar hand outside the chapter ring. The movement is signed by Riccard. 1660.* **£10,000**

◁ **PAIR-CASED POCKET WATCH** *Many watches of this period have decorative enamel dials. This piece is embellished with a frigate, and the numbers on the dial have been replaced by letters that spell out "Thomas Baldwin" – its owner. 1793; 2¼in across.* **£300**

△ **GOLD HUNTER-CASED WATCH**
Supposedly developed for use when hunting, the hunter case has a cover over the dial to protect both the dial and the glass. This cover *means that the intricate engraving on the backplate is concealed from the casual observer. Hunter-cased verge watches of this date are quite rare. 1820; 2in across.* **£450**

▷ **HALF-HUNTER WATCH**
The window in the case of this rather unusual silver verge watch shows that the case is a half-hunter. This aperture allows the hands, and the small chapter ring in the centre, to be seen at all times even when the case is closed. 1820; 2in across. **£150**

◁ **GOLD POCKET WATCH**
Made by the American company Elgin, this 9-carat gold gentleman's pocket watch is typical of the imported mass-produced pieces of the early 20th century. Gold watch chains are popular and this example is worth almost as much as the watch itself. 1900–05; 2¼in across. **£100–£150**

FOB & WRIST WATCHES

In the late 1800s, ladies started to wear watches as a type of brooch, suspended from a chain or strap. Sometimes the fob watch, as these were known, was mounted upside down to allow it to be more easily read.

The first wrist watches, small timepieces concealed in ladies' bracelets, date from the 1860s. They seemed rather effeminate to men, and wrist watches only became popular when their practicality was proven during World War I. Since then, the market for watches has been dominated by Swiss makers, such as Patek Philippe and Rolex.

SWISS ENAMELLED WATCH

Although painting with enamel developed in France, many of the best enamelled watch cases were made in Switzerland for export to the East. The enamelling on this gold watch shows a lady, whose clothes are set with tiny rose diamonds, on the front and flowers on the back. The case is set on both sides with split pearls, which shows that it was made for the Chinese market. 1890; 1¼in wide. **£750**

▷ **LADY'S FOB WATCH** *Made in the early 1900s, this gold watch combines the quality of American mass production (the movement is by the Waltham Watch Co.) with the Swiss tradition of fine decorative cases. The enamelled case is set with diamonds. c.1910; 1in across.* **£250–£300**

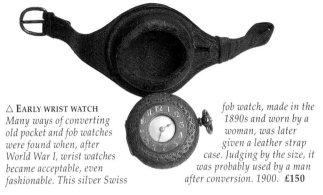

△ **EARLY WRIST WATCH**
Many ways of converting old pocket and fob watches were found when, after World War I, wrist watches became acceptable, even fashionable. This silver Swiss fob watch, made in the 1890s and worn by a woman, was later given a leather strap case. Judging by the size, it was probably used by a man after conversion. 1900. **£150**

△ **MINUTE-REPEATING WRIST WATCH**
When a small slide on the side of this 18-carat white gold watch is pushed it strikes the time to the last full minute. Such a complex mechanism is unusual – most repeating watches only mark the hour or quarter hour – and helps to make this watch very valuable. 1930s; Face 1¼in long. **£50,000**

▽ **COCKTAIL WATCH** *This attractive 1930s diamond-set platinum cocktail watch on a 9-carat white gold bracelet is true to the origins of the wrist watch as a piece of ladies' jewellery. 1935; Face ¾in long.* **£350**

COLLECTOR'S CHECKLIST

CLOCKS ARE SOME OF THE MOST interesting antiques, and one of the undoubted joys of owning a collection of timepieces is to be able to sit in a room and listen to the sound of several different clocks ticking away.

But most collectors are equally fascinated by the craftsmanship that goes into making a clock. The skills of a cabinet maker are required to make the case; of an horologist for the movement; of an engraver for the decoration and, often, of a gilder for the finishing touches. Watches can display even more amazing feats of engineering and have the advantage of taking up less space.

The fact that many clocks are items of furniture as well as mechanical devices dictates that any alterations that have been made must be thoroughly assessed before purchase. Small wheels that have been renewed do not usually affect the value, whereas a replacement dial is a matter of far greater importance and may severely reduce the worth.

Today, almost any longcase clock is something of a prized possession, and the days when certain types could be bought relatively cheaply are long gone. Anything costing less than £500 is now a true bargain, unless its condition is exceedingly poor, or it was made at a very late date.

High demand has meant that the faking of all clock types is common. Skeleton clocks, in particular, may be assembled from an assortment of clock parts. Fake patination can be achieved more easily on metal than wood,

and is often difficult for the new collector to spot. The only way to gain experience is to handle as many types of clock as possible.

There are three main ways of purchasing a clock or watch: at an auction; through a recognized dealer; or privately, from an individual. The auction houses in London have clock sales about six times a year, and they can be an exciting experience. Provincial sales are far more numerous. Great caution is advised, however, when buying at auction; both the piece and the sale catalogue should be carefully studied beforehand, and, if possible, expert advice should be sought.

Purchasing a good-quality timepiece through a reputable dealer is often a more expensive but much safer option, since any repairs or restoration work will almost certainly have been done to a high standard. Remember that only the best antiques prove to be good, long-term investments. If buying privately, always ask for a written statement detailing the piece's condition and history.

In general, new collectors would do well to seek friendly expert guidance when purchasing a clock or watch until their own level of experience increases. It can be easy, at first, to miss important details when trying to judge the worth of a piece. A second opinion may prove invaluable, since restoration work carried out on a poor-quality purchase, as well as often being costly, may still not enable you to achieve the full value of the same piece in perfect condition.

TIPS FOR BUYERS

1 It is important to establish that the movement and case of a clock belong together. Regard unexplained screw holes in either the case or movement with suspicion.

2 Always check that the dial of a longcase clock fits correctly into the case aperture and that the seat board has not been altered.

3 An original signature is important, particularly if it is the name of a well-known maker. It is, however, easy to change the signature on painted dials.

4 Original painted dials will show a network of tiny cracks, known as "crazing", even if they have been professionally cleaned and restored.

5 Replacement hands will be found on many clocks because of damage to the original hands. If the new hands are in the correct style and of the right quality, they will not detract from the value of the clock.

6 Check the running time of a clock; those that run for only 30 hours are generally less valuable than those that run for a full week or longer.

7 Make sure that watches are in working order since repairs can be prohibitively expensive.

8 Satisfy yourself that the case of a pocket watch labelled as "gold" really is gold. Some American makers produced cases of excellent quality in rolled gold (a type of plating in which thin sheets of gold are fused to a metal, such as copper, at high temperature, then rolled to form a sheet plated with a uniform thickness of gold).

9 Unless the movement is of particular interest to collectors, watches with cases made from 18-carat gold are more valuable than those of 9-carat gold. American manufacturers often used 14-carat gold for watch cases.

10 Waterproof watches may well have been opened for inspection, so if you buy a second-hand one, it is wise to have it resealed by a watchmaker.

COLLECTIONS OF INTEREST

Ashmolean Museum
Beaumont Street
Oxford OX1 2PH
Telephone: 01865 278 000

British Museum
Museum Street
London WC1B 3DG
Telephone: 0171 636 1555

Fitzwilliam Museum
Trumpington Street
Cambridge CB2 1RB
Telephone: 01223 332 900

Science Museum
Exhibition Street
London SW7 5BD
Telephone: 0171 938 8000

Victoria & Albert Museum
Cromwell Road
London SW7 2RL
Telephone: 0171 938 8500

Wallace Collection
Manchester Square
London W1M 6BN
Telephone: 0171 935 0687

Many fine examples of timepieces can also be seen in stately homes open to the public, as well as in provincial collections.

DOLLS, TOYS & GAMES

DOLLS, TOYS & GAMES

MADE TO LOVE, ENTERTAIN OR EDUCATE, TOYS have formed a part of everybody's childhood. All of us recognize with delight the toys from our own era. Some of us still carefully tend the dolls played with by our mothers and grandmothers, others wish we could find the doll of which such fond memories remain. It is understandable, then, that toys and dolls are so widely collected today, their shapes and faces stirring such deep memories within us.

The development of toys is linked closely to society's changing attitude toward children. Until the 18th century, children were regarded merely as small, naive adults. Children from aristocratic families were expected to amuse themselves as adults did, and miniature suits of armour and swords, for example, were provided for their entertainment. Children from the lower social orders were, of course, put to work at an early age, and their amusements would have been limited to whatever could be found; often this may have been nothing more than an inflated pig's bladder, which would have been patted about like today's balloons.

In the 18th century, the first books were produced commercially for children and it was discovered that a child could learn through play. Toward the end of the century, printed educational games and puzzles became available, which would, no doubt, have been sold in William Hamley's London toy shop, opened in 1760. Carved wooden toys such as tops, balls and Noah's arks were produced in southern Germany and were exported widely.

The Industrial Revolution created mechanized and inexpensive production techniques and led to machine-made toys of tin-plated sheet steel. Alongside this industrial growth was the emergence of the middle class, with enough money to demand machine-made toys and dolls for their children: the toy and doll industry was born.

Children 100 years ago were tempted by an enormous variety of toys: dolls with heads of porcelain, wax or papier mâché; wooden dolls' houses filled with painted tin-plate furniture; soft stuffed animals; the first toy railway; tin-plate and hand-painted vehicles and boats; and hollow-cast lead soldiers.

Toys were produced in great numbers between 1910 and the 1930s. Designers were quick to replicate real life in miniature and factories accurately reproduced each new technical advance: flying machines, submarines, underground railways and battle tanks. It is from this period that the earliest living memories date: of the streamlined saloon car with a clockwork motor, the pugnacious green tank locomotive, the golden teddy bear. But another toy first seen in the 1930s gained a huge audience of children worldwide – the Dinky Toy.

Produced in the first instance simply as accessories to enhance Hornby's railway layouts, Dinky Toys could be bought with pocket money and were up-to-the-minute designs of vehicles which any child might see any day in their own town. Toys at last were produced for the masses at affordable prices, and this concept has largely remained with manufacturers ever since.

Dolls
&
Soft Toys

Happy childhood memories of a
beloved doll or teddy draw many people
into collecting toys. Often charming, these
objects have now become very popular
and can prove to be valuable.
The best pieces, such as 18th-century
wooden dolls with their original clothes
or early Steiff teddy bears in perfect
condition, can fetch remarkably high
prices at auction. Over recent years,
the popularity of this field has
increased to the extent that almost any
prewar toy in good condition will attract
a collector. As with all antiques, the
most important consideration for
the buyer is the state of repair; although
well-loved but damaged toys may
be very appealing, they are
generally less valuable.

IDENTIFYING DOLLS

Many clues to a doll's age and origin are provided by the materials from which it is made, its body composition and shape. One of the most common types of old doll found today dates from 1915–25. They have bisque heads, with any makers' marks incised on the back.

These may be partly hidden, but by carefully easing up the wig at the back of the neck to expose the details, and by refer-ring to a book on doll trade-marks, amateurs can quite easily interpret the symbols.

For instance, those shown at **6** below can be deciphered as "F.S. & Co." (Franz Schmidt & Co.); "1272" (the mould refer-ence number, used *c*.1910); "58" (code for the size). "Deponiert" means that the maker claims registration. This information enables the doll to be quite accurately dated and valued.

DOLLS' HEADS

China heads, necks and shoulders (**1, 2**), popular in 1840–70, were usually German. Bisque heads (**3**) were common by the end of the 1880s. Eyes were made of glass in wax dolls (**4**) and bisque dolls; in the pressed felt dolls of the 1920s (**5**) they could be either glass or painted. Bisque dolls from the 1880s onward (**6**) usually bear makers' marks on the back of the head.

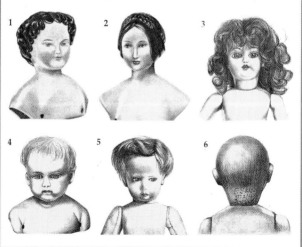

▽ **THREE DOLLS** *Until 1800, dolls were usually made of cloth, wood or wax, with the legs of most wooden dolls peg-jointed at the hip and knee. From 1800 to the 1870s, bodies tended to be made of* *shaped and padded kid or cloth, gusseted and seamed so they could be realistically posed. Bodies made of paper and wood pulp (1), with ball joints at hip, knee, shoulder and elbow, were used with bisque heads from the late 1870s. Bisque heads and composition "toddler bodies" (2), with curved limbs jointed only at the shoulder and hip, became popular after 1909. In 1900–20, celluloid (3) was used as a cheap alternative to bisque and composition; another cheap material was felt (see 2 below).*

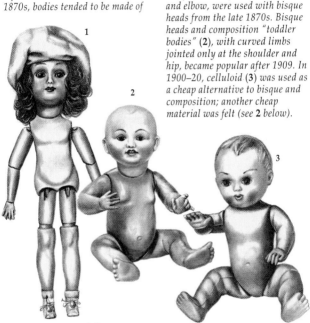

DOLLS' LIMBS

The limbs of early wooden dolls were made separately and slotted in. Early padded or kid dolls did not have articulated joints, but by the 1880s jointed composition bodies were common. Hands of kid stuffed with kapok (1) can be found on china and bisque shoulder dolls after *c.*1860. The 1920s felt doll (2) has stitched and padded hands, and the arms are jointed only at the shoulder.

Non-Bisque Dolls

The earliest dolls in many collections are wooden, with the head and body turned from a single piece of wood and the legs slotted into the bottom of the body; they date from the 1730s. Because their limbs are pegged together to allow movement, they are sometimes known as "peg" dolls.

The head, chest, lower arms and legs of wooden dolls are generally covered with gesso – a type of plaster – and then painted to resemble flesh. Originally the eyes were also painted, but in the 1700s black enamel eyes were inserted into the head to make them appear more lifelike.

By the 1830s, dolls made of papier mâché, which could be moulded by machine, were being produced in large numbers in Germany and exported all over

Europe. Wax, too, which can be easily shaped, was used in several ways to make dolls' heads or "shoulder heads", where the head and shoulders were cast together.

Wax gives the most natural-looking features, but it is soft, difficult to work with and expensive, so it was a long time before it was deemed to be suitable for mere toys.

▷ **George III wooden doll** *This unusual English doll has rouged cheeks, inserted black eyes without pupils, feathered brows and a blonde wig. Her waist is tapered to rounded hips, her legs end in block feet, and she has wooden forearms, with long, bent fingers. c.1790; 13½in tall.*
£800–£1,200

▽ **PAPIER MÂCHÉ DOLLS** *The 18½-inch standing doll is a papier mâché shoulder head doll, whose dark, plaited wig hides a black-painted head. She was made in Germany c.1850.* **£500–£700**
The unusually tall seated doll measures 27 inches. She was also made in Germany – at the end of the 19th century – and has two moulded lower teeth, fixed blue glass eyes and a mohair wig. **£300–£500**

▷ **WAXED-COMPOSITION SHOULDER HEAD DOLL** *with a cloth body and wooden lower arms. She has fixed glass eyes and a wig made from real hair. Her mouth is open and she has both upper and lower teeth. She still wears her original clothes. c.1865; 19in tall.* **£300–£500**

WAX DOLLS

The heyday of wax-doll making was from the early 1800s to the 1930s. The wax used was beeswax, bleached, coloured and strengthened with additives. Dolls are of three types: solid wax (these tend to be older and smaller and are rarer), poured wax and wax over composition or papier mâché.

The main drawback to wax over composition is that the thin layer of wax expands and contracts at a different rate from the composition and so is prone to cracking, which does affect the value.

Eyes and hair varied according to the type of doll. The eyes of a solid wax doll were painted on or were glass attached by molten wax. Most poured wax dolls had proper eye sockets, with glass eyes attached to the inside of the head. The heads of wax over composition dolls were strong enough to take the weight of eyes that opened and closed, which were also fixed inside the head.

The simplest hair was carved or moulded; wigs were made by attaching human hair or mohair to a cloth base. Sometimes hair was inserted into small slits all over the head and the slits resealed. Some wax over composition dolls had a clump of hair inserted into a single large slit on top of the head.

◁ **ENGLISH POURED WAX DOLL** *with wax lower arms and legs, a cloth body and hair inserted into the head in clumps. The brown stain on her face is the result of ageing. She still has her original clothes and bonnet. c.1880; 16in tall.*
£400–£600

△ **WAXED-COMPOSITION DOLLS** *These German slit-head dolls have mohair ringlets, cloth bodies and kid forearms. Such pairs with similar or matching clothes are extremely unusual. c.1840; 21in tall.* The pair **£500–£700**

CLOTH AND KID BODIES

Most wax dolls have kid or cloth bodies. They were made in sections, of calico stuffed with cow hair or sawdust, and were then stitched together. The wax head and shoulders were always made as one piece, with holes at the back and front (often reinforced with metal eyelets) so that they could be stitched to the torso.

In the 1850s, the German maker Charles Motschmann patented "floating" limbs, in which the upper arms, upper legs and midriff were made from unstuffed cloth tubes.

▽ **CLOTH BODIES WITH LITTLE SHAPE** *tended to be used for baby dolls. Like most wax dolls, the head, lower legs and lower arms were of wax over composition.*

◁ **KID WAS OFTEN USED** *to model the curvaceous shapes of French fashion dolls. Gussets were used on kid bodies at elbows and knees to allow more realistic posing of the limbs.*

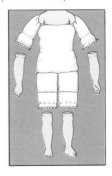

French Bisque Dolls

During the 18th century, France gained a reputation for fine-quality dolls, but by the early 1800s the French faced fierce competition from English wax dolls and, after 1830, from papier mâché dolls that were mass produced in Germany.

After 1840, several French makers, including companies such as Jumeau, Gaultier and Bru began producing bisque dolls of great beauty (in 1842, 1860 and 1866 respectively).

Two types of doll were commonly made: the bébé and the lady doll, or Parisienne, whose golden age was the 1860s and 1870s. These lady dolls usually have a bisque shoulder head

▷ JUMEAU FASHION DOLL
Such dolls as this bisque Parisienne with a swivel head are highly prized by collectors. She has a closed mouth, fixed blue eyes and a blonde mohair wig over a cork pate. Her body is leather, with separately stitched fingers, and she is dressed in the height of fashion in a finely embroidered cream on beige silk taffeta dress with a matching hat, leather shoes and silk stockings.
c.1875; 18in tall.
£4,000–£5,000

stitched on to a kid body, with the lower arms and legs often made of porcelain.

The high-quality bisque heads usually have large and lustrous blown-glass eyes, which gives them a particularly lifelike quality. The mouths are closed, the ears are often pierced, with earrings, and the dolls have real hair or mohair wigs in an elaborate coiffure.

The Parisiennes were finely dressed dolls seen not only as playthings but also as models for the latest French fashions.

▷ "MADAME BARROIS"
A swivel-head lady doll with fixed blue glass eyes, pierced ears and a blonde mohair wig over a cork pate. She has a gusseted kid body, her fingers are separately stitched and she is wearing her original silk gown with a bustle and brown button boots. c.1852; 15in tall. **£2,500–£3,500**

▷ BÉBÉ DOLLS *were made to represent small children. Their bodies are usually wood and composition with eight joints and straight wrists, as with this Jumeau doll. She has fixed blue glass eyes, applied pierced ears and a brown mohair wig over a cork pate. Her dress and shoes are not original. 1875; 23in tall.* **£2,000–£3,000**

German Bisque Dolls

For about 90 years, from the mid-1800s, the most popular material for dolls' heads was bisque – a once-fired, unglazed porcelain made from kaolin, which gave a matt finish. A plentiful supply of kaolin and a large, poorly paid workforce in Germany ensured that, between 1870 and 1940, millions of bisque dolls were made there and exported all over the world.

Early dolls had moulded hair and fixed glass eyes. Later, the heads were tinted in flesh tones, and the dolls were given mohair or real hair wigs and gravity-operated "sleeping" eyes.

Dolls' bodies were mainly papier mâché, although some were made of bisque and these are known as "all bisque" dolls. As is common elsewhere, the

◁ **Early bisque doll**
made by Simon & Halbig. The company started in 1870, but this unmarked shoulder head doll was probably made later. She wears her original fine wool clothes, which have remained immaculate because the doll has been kept in a box. c.1880; 16in tall. **£400–£600**

Types of Mouth

1 Closed A small, slightly pursed mouth with a full lower lip found on early ceramic dolls.

2 Open Developed to give the face a more natural, smiling expression. The upper teeth and tongue may be visible.

3 Open/Closed A painted mouth which appears to be open but is not.

identification marks for maker, mould number and size are usually found either on the back of the doll's head or on the shoulder plate.

MAKERS OF BISQUE DOLLS
Armand Marseille; Bahr & Proschild; Gebrüder Heubach; Heubach Koppelsdorf; J.D. Kestner; Kammer & Reinhardt; Schoenau & Hoffmeister; Simon & Halbig

◁ **A CHARMING DOLL** *which has been given a new body and dress. She has a very good head, however, and is consequently valuable. She was made by the popular makers Gebrüder Heubach and bears the mould number 8192. c.1914; 12in tall.* **£150–250**

THE MOST EXPENSIVE DOLL IN THE WORLD

On February 8, 1994, a 25¼-inch bisque-headed doll was sold at Sotheby's in London, for the world record price of £190,000. She was made by Kammer & Reinhardt, mould no. 108, and is the only example discovered to date. It is possible that 108 was an experimental mould. It was modelled as a particular child with a wistful, half-smiling expression, very different to the faces of the majority of German bisque dolls seen today which were made in huge numbers. Character faces are generally more unusual and sought after.

△ **A DOLL**, *probably made by Simon & Halbig, with a toddler's body and the number 914 on the back of her head. Rather than the normal bland expression, she has what is described as a "character" face. c.1915; 14in tall.* **£250–£350**

DOLLS' FURNITURE

Most collector look for dolls' house furniture dating from the 1880s. There is no standard size for such furniture, and pieces from an inch to a foot in height are all classed as dolls' house, or miniature, furniture.

A variety of materials was used, including wood, metal, bone and tortoiseshell, and the detail is often superb. Types include carved bone items from India, Viennese gilt-metal pieces with enamel decoration and French pieces with carved wooden legs and silk upholstery. Wooden pieces painted with gold to simulate boulle inlay, from Walthershausen, Germany, are specially prized.

△ THIS SECRETAIRE, *made in Germany, shows a wealth of detail: it is decorated with gold scrollwork, the pigeonholes are flanked by two small cupboards, and three crowns ornament the cornice. c.1890; 6½in high.* **£250–£350**

▷ DRESSING-TABLE MIRROR
A beautifully made mirror in high-quality walnut with many period details including mouldings and bun feet. c.1880; 5in high. **£200–£300**

◁ **UPHOLSTERED CHAIR** *with a stained wood frame and turned legs. It is part of a set comprising armchairs, sofa (see bottom) and table, all ornately painted in gold scrollwork to resemble brass inlay. c.1880; 5in high.* **£50–£70**

▽ **WOOD-FRAME SOFA,** *upholstered in olive-green silk. The pale wood has been well carved and stained to resemble cherry. Originally there were four matching armchairs and a table. c.1890; 9in wide.* **£60–£80**

▷ **UPHOLSTERED SOFA** *in stained wood, with a carved back painted with gold scrollwork to resemble boulle. c.1880; 5in high.* **£50–£70**

Interest in collecting miniature furniture has grown over the past few years – whether for furnishing dolls' houses or for display. Even items made fairly recently, such as plastic furniture and crockery, have their own following with collectors.

A large number of functional items – kitchen equipment and china, for instance – are available, but decorative pieces, including hand-painted pictures in gilt-metal frames, are rarer and tend to fetch higher prices when they come to auction.

Articles that are hard to come by, such as birdcages, sewing machines and clocks, can command as much as £100 each.

Doll's Pram

This piece is very closely modelled on the full-size perambulators which

would have been seen in Victorian cities in the 1890s. Made of painted wood with a padded interior, the pram has sprung suspension and is supported by delicate spoked wheels. Prams of this scale appeal to two groups of collectors: doll accessory collectors; and those who are interested in prams in their own right. 1890s. **£250–£300**

▷ **PINE TABLE** stained to resemble oak. Although it was made in England, the legs are intricately carved in 17th-century Dutch style. The copper and aluminium jelly moulds are contemporary. c.1910; 4in high. **£80–£120**

◁ **COUNTRY KITCHEN** The table and chairs were made during World War II by a soldier serving in Burma; the pottery teapot, jugs and plate are from the same time. The other objects were all made in Germany in the 1890s. 5in high. **£120–£200**

△ **MINIATURE FOOD TINS** Made in Germany, this selection of containers for, among other things, cocoa, tea, salt and oats is transfer-printed in bright designs. c.1890; 2in high. The set **£50–£70**

▽ **TIN-PLATE COOKING RANGE** This is too big for a dolls' house and was probably meant as a toy for a child. The range is complete with methylated spirit heater, chimney with copper top, paw feet, a kettle and four cooking pots. c.1910; 13in wide. **£200–£300**

TEDDY BEARS

Soft bears on all fours were made before 1900 and the first with movable joints in 1902, but it was not until 1906 that the teddy bear got its name.

Up to the 1920s, teddy bears looked fiercer than the cuddly teddies of today, for their features were modelled on the grizzly and brown bears. Until the 1930s, when bright scarlet, blue, purple and yellow bears appeared, their coats were natural in colour.

Initially, teddies were filled with excelsior (wood shavings) or a mixture of kapok and excelsior; later they were stuffed with kapok alone.

The best-known maker is the German company, Steiff. Other teddy-making firms include: Chad Valley, Merrythought and Pedigree in England; Schuco and Fleischmann & Bloedal in Germany; and the Ideal Novelty and Toy Company in the U.S.

△ **STEIFF BUTTONS** *Many of the most valuable bears were made by the German company Steiff, whose bears can be identified by a small metal button in the left ear. The design of the buttons has changed over the years and can, if they are in a good enough condition, be used for dating. Designs have included an elephant and the word "Steiff". Imitation buttons are now being made, so it may be useful to examine a genuine button before starting a collection.*

HOW TEDDY GOT HIS NAME

President Theodore "Teddy" Roosevelt was a keen hunter. In 1902 a cartoon appeared showing Roosevelt refusing to shoot a bear cub. The cartoon was well received and the bear cub was used in other cartoons of Roosevelt. At the same time, soft toy bears were being imported from Germany. They soon became popular with Roosevelt's adult followers and by 1906 the toys were known as "Teddy Bears".

◁ **STEIFF TEDDY** *Shown together with a photograph of his original owners, this fine gold plush teddy bear has the Steiff button in his ear. He has a humped back and is stuffed with excelsior. c.1908; 11in tall.* **£600–£800**

◁ **YES/NO TEDDY BY SCHUCO** *The tail of this gold bear is linked to his head – moving the tail turns the head from side to side and up and down. The loss of his ears, eyes and pads affects his value. 1925; 15in tall.* **£200–£300**

GUIDE FOR BUYERS

When collecting old teddy bears it is important to note that only those that can be identified as having been made by a particular firm and are in good condition are of any value.

▷ **GOLD PLUSH TEDDY** *This bear was made by Merrythought, an English toy-making company which was established in 1930 at Ironbridge in Shropshire. With his plastic nose, glass eyes and velvet pads with embroidered claws he is a good example of the well-made teddies Merrythought is known for. c.1950; 21in tall.* **£80–£120**

△▷ **SOMERSAULTING BEAR**
The unusual feature of this fine blond plush bear with his black boot-button eyes is his ability to turn somersaults. An internal mechanism means that when his arms are wound, he flips over. Made by the German firm Gebrüder Bing before World War I, this type of teddy is rare. c.1913; 13½in tall. **£400–£600**

FEARSOME TEDDY

Over the last decade, teddy bears have become very popular with collectors. Although well-cuddled teddies are often the most endearing, they may be almost worthless. It is the bears in mint condition, and particularly those that are somewhat unusual, that are prized by collectors and fetch huge sums at auction.

This splendid 22-inch tall blond plush teddy is a fine example. He was made by Steiff, the most sought-after teddy maker, *c.*1908, has a brown stitched nose, a humped back and a growler in his stomach. He would fetch more than £5,000 at auction today.

▽ **MUSICAL BEAR** *Halfway down the back of this teddy is a key that winds up a mechanism operating a musical movement inside. Made by Schuco, a popular German toy maker, this teddy bear has gold plush "fur", black glass eyes, a hump back, a metal rod attaching the head to the body and swivelling joints. c.1925; 22in tall.* **£300–£500**

SOFT TOYS

Although some soft toys were made earlier, it was only in the 1890s that serious production of fabric animals and figures began.

They were generally made from felt, plush, velvet, printed cotton or fur cloth and were filled with kapok, excelsior (fine wood shavings), granulated cork and sometimes even sawdust.

Magarete Steiff, a German toy maker, was the first to make soft animals on a commercial scale. Still active today, her company is best known for its teddy bears, although it manufactured a variety of animals and dolls. All its toys were made of plush, felt

△ **MICKEY AND MINNIE MOUSE** *were both produced in England by Dean's Rag Book Company. Made of velvet and cotton, they are large and quite unusual. If they were in good condition, clean and with tails, their value could be twice as high. 1930s; 14in high seated.* **£600–£800**

◁ **DOPEY** *This amusing velvet Dopey, with his painted face, was made for the promotion of Walt Disney's* Snow White and the Seven Dwarfs *in 1937. 10in high.* **£300–£400**

◁ **SCHUCO BULLY BULLDOG** *is made from good orange and white plush. He has brown-tipped hair and is wearing a leather collar. The most popular animals for soft toys included dogs, cats, rabbits, lions, tigers, pigs and elephants. c.1927; 12in tall.* **£300–£400**

or mohair fur and marked with the distinctive Steiff button.

In the 1920s, another German firm, Schuco, began producing soft animals. These often had a clockwork movement or a wire link between the head and tail which turned the head as the tail was moved.

English factories also started to make soft toys: Dean's began production in 1903; Chad Valley and Norah Wellings in the 1920s; Merrythought in 1930 and Pedigree in 1942. The toys were marked by various means such as sewn-on labels, printed or woven tags, or names stencilled or stamped on the fabric.

The value of soft toys is particularly dependent upon their condition. Once badly stained or worn, they become almost impossible to repair.

△ **FELIX THE CAT** *The black-and-white plush cat on the right has felt ears, glass eyes and a humped back. His companion is made of felt and has a ribbon and squeaker. 1920s; 14in tall (right), 12in tall (left).* Each **£200–£300**

◁ **FELT ELEPHANT** *The four metal wheels allow this early Steiff toy to roll along. He also has a press squeaker in his belly. c.1897; 16in long.* **£350–£500**

Toy
Figures

Collecting toy figures, including such
diverse playthings as model soldiers,
space travellers and clockwork animals,
is becoming increasingly popular.
The term "antique toys" can be
misleading, since many are less than
100 years old. Indeed, most of the toys in
this section were made between the
1890s and 1940s, when factory
production became established.
Germany, America and Britain led the
world in manufacturing toy figures,
although many later examples, such
as the space toys which date mainly from
the 1950s and '60s, were made in Japan.
With the exception of some
lead soldiers, which can be expensive
and are much sought after, toy
figures, especially those made after
World War II, offer the new enthusiast
a relatively cheap and plentiful
source of collectables.

TOY SOLDIERS

Model soldiers have a long history, stretching back thousands of years. In ancient Egypt they were used to represent armies in the pharaohs' tombs, and Roman children are known to have played with figures of soldiers.

Solid and flat-cast lead soldiers have been popular for a few hundred years, but the mass production of lead alloy figures began only in 1893,

when the company William Britain & Sons perfected the hollow-cast method. Although makers such as Johillco and Reka Ltd. copied its methods, Britains was responsible for more than half the lead soldiers produced. It was only with the introduction of cheaper plastic figures in the 1960s that production diversified.

Although they are unmarked, the earliest figures from Britains,

△ **ROYAL HORSE ARTILLERY "W" SERIES** *Made by Britains, this set, no. 125, comes complete with its original box and is in good condition. Figures in the "W" series are smaller than standard size. c.1938; 2in high.* **£100–£120**

▷ **MILITARY BAND FIGURES** *The bugler in khaki dress was made by Johillco (John Hill & Co.), while the later drummer is from a nine-piece Britains set called "Bands of the Line". 1914–20; 2in high.* Each **£5–£8** (in mint condition **£10–£15**)

those with oval bases, can be identified by the high quality of the casting and painting. Great care was taken to ensure that uniforms, weapons and colours were correct. After 1900, paper labels were stuck to the bases to protect copyright, and from about 1905 cast lettering was used. Figures produced after 1907 had square bases.

The condition of toy soldiers is all-important, and an original box in good condition can double the price of a set. Beware of any damage or repainting which can significantly affect the value of a lead soldier.

△ **SOLID-CAST FIGURES** *These soldiers from the Napoleonic era include a standard-bearer, a fusilier and a mounted officer. They were all probably made by the Heyde factory in Dresden, Germany. 1895–1900; 2½in high.* Officer £10–£15; Infantry £5–£10

▽ **AN AMBULANCE WAGON** *of the Royal Army Medical Corps made by Britains, set no. 145. An earlier and more valuable version of this set is identifiable by its grey wagon, heavier collar harness and by flatter horses' ears. c.1924; 3½in high.* **£150–£200**

SPACE TOYS

When the first Sputnik satellite was launched in 1957, it heralded the beginning of the Space Age. This exciting new era not only influenced the design of cars and fabrics but also inspired the science fiction and space fantasy markets.

Comic strips featured such heroes as Buck Rogers and Dan Dare, and Hollywood made more films about space. The earliest space toys were actually produced as promotional spin-offs from these films. With the advent of television, more toys were inspired by programmes like *Space 1999* and *Fireball XL5*.

During the 1960s, the heyday of space toys, most were made

△ **Moon Explorer Vehicle** *Both the rocket-shaped remote-control unit and the vehicle itself are in mint condition. It was made by* Yonezawa and comes complete with lights, motor sound, moving antennae and its original box. 1960s; 8½in long. **£120–£200**

by Japanese companies, usually of lithographed tin plate with plastic or Perspex detailing.

As this type of toy was made fairly recently and generally in large numbers, their condition is of paramount importance to the collector. High prices are only paid for toys in mint condition and preferably in their original boxes.

△ **MANOEUVRES IN SPACE** *These brightly coloured spacecraft were made by the Masudaya company. Their value is increased by the presence of the circling space walker. Such figures are rare since they have usually become detached over the years. 1960s; 8½in long (left).* Together **£200–£300**

◁ **TWO SPACECRAFT** *Both of these battery-powered toys have survived in excellent condition, a fact reflected in their value. The "Mars" spaceship (left), was made by Masudaya, while Yoshia made the spacerocket. 1960s; 14½in (left) and 13½in.* The pair **£250–£350**

ROBOTS & ASTRONAUTS

Recent years have seen mechanical robot figures become popular collectables. These ingenious toys, inspired by the growing interest in space travel and science fiction since the 1950s, often now command high prices at auction.

Initially, Japan was the leading producer of toy robots. Companies such as Bandai, Linemar, Nomura and Alps

△ **PLASTIC DALEK** *A battery-powered model, available in silver or black, that was highly popular in the late '60s. A more accurate tin-plate version was made by Codeg. 6in high.* **£100–£150**

◁ **"DUX ROBOT ASTROMAN"** *Rare plastic figure made in Germany by Markes & Co. It is operated by a four-function remote control and the mechanism is visible inside its plastic chest. Late 1950s; 12in tall.* **£600–£700**

exported large numbers of tin-plate models in the 1950s and '60s, and plastic models from the '60s onward. Post-1960s battery-powered figures from Japan are highly collectable.

The best-known British robots are the Daleks, from BBC TV's *Doctor Who*. Although popular all over the world, most Dalek toys – both metal and plastic – were manufactured in Britain; those produced by Codeg during the 1960s are considered to be the finest.

New robots are generally battery powered and made of plastic. Tin-plate pieces, based on 1960s and '70s models from Japan and Europe, are still being made today in China and the former Soviet Union. Such items are a cheaper alternative to collecting older toy robots.

Before purchasing a battery-operated robot, remember to check for corrosion from acid leaks. The number of lights and moving parts does not affect value, and an original box is always a bonus.

◁ **RARE WALKING ROBOT ASTRONAUT** *The laser gun rises up to fire but the antenna on top of the helmet is missing. This tin-plate toy was made in Japan but, since its box is missing and it is unmarked, the maker is unknown. 1955; 10in tall.* **£300–£400**

▷ **TIN-PLATE "ROBOTANK Z"** *by Nomura of Tokyo. The eyes and the light between the two guns flash on and off, and the arms (each holding a lever) move, giving the effect of self-propulsion. 1960s; 10in tall.* **£100–£150**

ANIMAL TOYS

Noah's Arks are among the earliest wooden toys. Sometimes with more than 100 animals, they were highly popular in the 19th century. This type of toy was approved of by adults because of its religious associations.

With increased popularity of animal models as playthings, William Britain & Sons launched their lead farm animals in 1923. Farmyard accessories, zoo and circus animals followed. These detailed pieces are now fairly inexpensive to collect. Fox hunting sets were also produced.

When tin was introduced, lead toy making declined. Most tin-plate toys tend to be mechanical and are known as "novelty" pieces.

◁ **ELEPHANT "RINGMASTER"**
A celluloid clockwork elephant in a painted uniform and in such good condition is a rare find. 1920s; 7in high.
£150–£180

▽ **CAST-IRON HORSE AND CART**
Farmyard sets with accessories, such as haystacks and troughs, are particularly valuable. c.1900; 4in long. **£40–£60**

△ **WOODEN ELEPHANT**
This movable piece is from the "Humpty Dumpty Circus" made by the Schoenhut company. c.1925; 8in high. **£30–£40**

NOAH'S ARK

Bavaria was the most prolific producer of arks in Europe. Much sought after today, an early ark in good condition and containing around one hundred pairs of animals can fetch as much as £4,000. Flat-bottomed arks are not as collectable as the boat-shaped variety. This example, even complete with 72 figures is only worth £800.

An ark's animals and figures were individually hand-carved until the early 19th century, when they were sliced off a large carved ring of wood.

▽ *In the ring method a rough outline was carved into a block. When sliced, this produced animals of uniform size which were then finished by hand.*

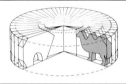

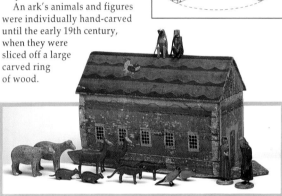

▽ **NOAH'S ARK FIGURES**
These models were made from Elastolin – a mixture of gum arabic, chalk and sawdust – by the German company Elastolin. 1930s; 1in–6in high. **£500**

Automata

When wound up, these mechanical amusements, known as automata, imitate the movement of a person or animal. They were essentially intended for adults, but of course also appealed to children.

The first true automata, incredibly intricate figures or animals with complex movements, were made in the 18th century. They were large and complicated, which made them expensive. In response to this, factories and workshops began to make smaller cheaper figures. Most of these were clockwork, although some later pieces were powered by electricity.

Fakes have recently appeared on the market and can be hard to spot. Check under the clothes to make sure the figure looks old and beware of tempting offers that seem too good to be true.

△ **MONKEY PLAYING THE FIDDLE**
Many of the best automata were made by French companies. This monkey, playing a fiddle in the garden of a chateau, was made by Phalibois. c.1875; 16in high.
£1,500–£2,000

◁ **"THE MARRIAGE PROPOSAL"** *This type of picture automaton was most commonly made in France. They reached the height of their popularity around the turn of the century.*

Once wound up, many parts of the scene are set in motion – figures pop up and down and eyes and limbs move. c.1900; 11in high. **£400–600**

▽ **DANCING PUNCHINELLO** *When the handle is turned, this amusing French-made doll dances while music plays from an internal movement. Hand-wound toys were originally cheaper than clockwork versions. c.1885; 11in high.* **£600–£900**

△ **NAUTICAL SCENE** *When set in motion the small doll on the shore waves at the ship being buffeted by heavy seas. c.1890; 16in high.* **£800–£1,200**

▽ **MUSICAL GROUP** *These highly collectable figures were not made as a set. The pigs were marketed as "Walt Disney's Three Little Pigs". The girl conductor was made separately. c.1935; 5in high. The group* **£500–£700**

NOVELTY TOYS

The term "novelty toys" encompasses a wide variety of pieces and includes amusing representations of figures from contemporary life and characters from films, fables and books.

Until the mid-20th century most of these tin-plate toys were both manufactured and sold in Europe. The most important toy makers of the time included: the big German manufacturers Märklin, Carette, Gunthermann, Bing and Plank, who are better known for their trains and road vehicles; other German toy makers Lehmann, Schuco, Adams and Stock; the French company Martin; and the American firm Marx.

△ **CAT AND MOUSE TOY** *Known as "Nina", this clockwork toy was made by Lehmann. The tin body has been painted and sprayed with a type of flock. It is unfortunate in terms of the value that the original box is not in better condition. 1920s; 7in long.* **£500–£600**

◁ **GOOFY THE GARDENER** *Disney characters, such as this one, are very popular with collectors. Goofy was made in both America and Britain by Louis Marx. 1935–40; 4in high.* **£150–£180**

The outbreak of World War II seriously disrupted the European toy-making industry, and when the Japanese started production, soon after 1945, they quickly became dominant.

In the 19th and early 20th centuries, most toys were powered by either a clockwork spring, a motor or steam. As this century has progressed, new forms of propulsion have been devised, including battery power, friction drive and gyroscopes.

▷ **TIN-PLATE BALLERINA**
A tiny gyroscope inside the foot of this fine German-made ballerina allows her to remain poised on one leg. 1950s; 5in tall. **£50–£80**

▽ **COCKEREL AND EGG CART** *This tin-plate clockwork toy was made by Lehmann in Germany and is known as the "Duo". Although it is scratched and the axle has been repaired, the piece is rare and is therefore still quite valuable. Lehmann was founded in 1881 in Brandenburg by Ernst Lehmann and is regarded as one of the best producers of novelty toys. 1930s; 6¾in long.* **£480–£550**

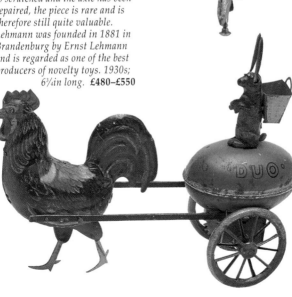

VEHICLES, TRAINS & CONSTRUCTION SETS

Model trains, cars, boats and
planes from earlier decades are hugely
popular with collectors. Since the
demand for these toys is high, many
enthusiasts specialize in collecting a
particular type, such as die-cast or tin-
plate vehicles; or a famous make,
such as Dinky model cars and
lorries or Hornby train sets.
Before World War I, production
was dominated by a small number of
German companies, including Märklin,
Bing and Carette, which exported
their toys around the world. The rarity
and quality of their pieces mean that
they are particularly valued by collectors.
The best prices are paid for scarce
items in "mint and boxed" condition,
that is, as they left the factory.

MODEL BOATS

Some of the most familiar types of model boat are the tin-plate variety. These water-going boats are powered by clockwork, steam or electricity. The most sought-after models are early 20th-century liners and battleships by such German toy makers as Bing, Carette, Märklin and Fleishmann.

Another important category of model boat is scale models of working vessels. They were made by skilled amateurs, often by sailors in their spare time, and range from simple fishing smacks to oil tankers. Intended for display rather than for use, some of the best examples of these wooden scale models are the finely detailed frigates and other war ships made by French prisoners during the Napoleonic Wars.

▽ **GUNBOAT** *The German company Carette, which made this tin-plate clockwork model, supplied the English company Bassett-Lowke with many of its models. In fact, this boat flies the Union Jack on both its masts. c.1904; 20in long.* **£600–£800**

△ **"LEVIATHAN"** *Tin-plate boats are prone to rusting, which means that well-preserved pieces are more valuable. This liner, made by Bing, is a fine example since its masts, propellors and paintwork are all intact. c.1920; 13in long.* **£400–£600**

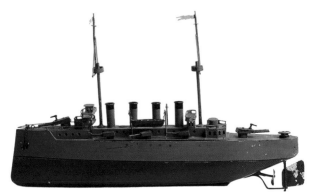

Dinky's colourful "waterline" series of warships and liners made in the 1930s and '40s are a lesser category of collectable model boats. These small ships are distinguished by being keel-less and flat-bottomed.

Much rarer and more keenly desired are large-scale models of naval and merchant vessels professionally engineered by shipyard apprentices. Such models were typically presented to the shipyard owners and many are now on display in museums. Knowing the history of the ship represented is an added bonus for enthusiasts.

△ **"SS MASCOT"** *This remarkably detailed ship was constructed by an amateur, probably a member of the crew. The vessel's interior from wheelhouse to engine room is revealed layer by layer as the decks are removed. The details on each section are accurate and include buckets and a working compass.*
c.1910; 3ft 1in long. **£1,000–£1,200**

◁ **BATTLESHIP** *made in tin plate by Bing. Pre-World War I German models, though never made to scale and often lacking detail, are highly sought after. Most are clockwork powered, but other examples, such as this, are driven by steam.*
c.1912; 30in long. **£500–£700**

TIN-PLATE VEHICLES

Children's toys often mirror contemporary society. This is especially true of model vehicles. As modes of transport changed, so did the miniature versions made for children. Indeed, part of their fascination for collectors is as a memento of a world that has disappeared.

The first tin-plate vehicles were made in the early 19th century in Germany. They were generally cut out individually from large sheets of tin-plated steel, which were then shaped, soldered and painted by hand.

Around 1908, tin-plate toys began to be decorated using the offset lithography process. This involved printing both the design and the decoration on flat sheets of metal, which were then cut and shaped by machine. Small metal tabs were used to hold the toys together. This mechanization allowed the toys to be made in larger numbers and far more cheaply.

△ **SMART SALOON CAR** *Complete with battery-operated lights, a uniformed driver and doors and a boot that open, this clockwork car was made by Tipp & Co. Founded in 1912 in Nuremberg, Tipp & Co. was known for its large-scale tin-plate cars. 1930s; 20½in long.*
£800–£1,200

▽ **LIMOUSINE BY BING** *The rear doors of this limousine by the German manufacturer Gebrüder Bing open. The car runs on a clockwork mechanism and has a driver. 1920s; 10½in long.*
£600–£900

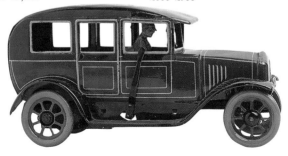

TIN-PLATE MOTORBUS

Patented by the German toy maker Ernst Lehmann in 1907, this 8-inch-long motorbus is a fine copy of a vehicle that was very common at the time. Its features include a uniformed driver and a staircase to the top deck; it is powered by a ratchet and spring mechanism. In excellent condition a bus like this is worth between £1,200 and £1,500.

▽▷ *The ratchet and spring mechanism is visible when the bus is turned over.*

▽ *The dumbbell is the Lehmann trademark. The metal construction tabs can be seen beside the wheels.*

△ *Beneath the front, the axle, which is connected to the steering wheel, can be seen. Note that the tin has been marked "Lehmann".*

German companies dominated both the production and export of tin-plate toys during the late 1800s and early 1900s. They even adapted their products to different countries using subtly varied colour schemes and lettering. The best German makers were Bing, Carette, Gunthermann, Märklin and Plank. As time passed, their dominance was challenged by British, French and American companies.

After World War I, British toy makers started to produce tin-plate pieces. The major names include Hornby (and Meccano which was made by Hornby), Lines Brothers (later Tri-ang), Chad Valley, Wells, Burnett and James Walker.

Tin-plate toys remained popular until the mid-1930s when the cheaper die-cast toys entered the market.

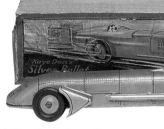

△ **KAYE DON'S SILVER BULLET**
Built to commemorate Kaye Don's attempt on the world land-speed record in 1930. It was made by the German firm Gunthermann in lithographed tin plate. 1930; 22in long. **£650–£850**

△ **GROUP OF TIN-PLATE CARS** *Even relatively modern mass-produced tin-plate vehicles can be valuable if in good condition; those that have been well used are often virtually worthless. Models that were produced in limited numbers also tend to be more valuable.*

1 *Open-top cruiser complete with box. c.1955; 13in long.* **£180–£250**. **2** *Racing car. c.1955; 9½in long.* **£120–£200**. **3** *Small bus. c.1955; 4½in long.* **£10–£15**. **4** *Open-top tourer. c.1955; 9in long.* **£80–£120**. **5** *Racing car. c.1935; 12in long.* **£80–£120**.

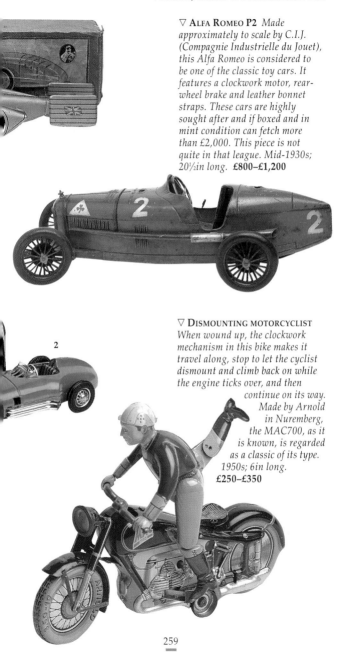

▽ **ALFA ROMEO P2** *Made approximately to scale by C.I.J. (Compagnie Industrielle du Jouet), this Alfa Romeo is considered to be one of the classic toy cars. It features a clockwork motor, rear-wheel brake and leather bonnet straps. These cars are highly sought after and if boxed and in mint condition can fetch more than £2,000. This piece is not quite in that league. Mid-1930s; 20½in long.* **£800–£1,200**

▽ **DISMOUNTING MOTORCYCLIST** *When wound up, the clockwork mechanism in this bike makes it travel along, stop to let the cyclist dismount and climb back on while the engine ticks over, and then continue on its way. Made by Arnold in Nuremberg, the MAC700, as it is known, is regarded as a classic of its type. 1950s; 6in long.* **£250–£350**

DIE-CAST VEHICLES

The appeal of die-cast vehicles, the most widely collected toys today in Britain, is due partly to the nostalgia collectors feel for the toys they played with when they were children and partly to the availability of such toys.

By the process of die-casting, huge numbers of cars, lorries and aeroplanes could be made inexpensively from a reusable mould. Various companies used slightly different materials for their toys, but most were lead based. They were finished in lead-based paints and could be produced far more cheaply than the lithographed tin-plate toys popular at the time.

To be of maximum value today, die-cast toys must be in perfect condition and still in their own original boxes.

In 1934, fired by the success of "Tootsietoys" from America in the early 1930s, the British Meccano company, part of the Hornby empire, pioneered its own range of die-cast model

vehicles known as Dinky Toys. These were first intended simply as accessories to the successful O-gauge train sets Hornby was already making in quantity. Their popularity soon equalled that of the trains, however, and the company was quick to realize the value of these toys as playthings in their own right.

During World War II, toy production ceased, but by 1946 the Meccano company was again issuing a wide range of cars, vans, lorries, aeroplanes and ships. Some were reissues of old models, but many were new.

▽ RARE SET OF DINKY MECHANICAL "HORSES" *with detachable trailers in the liveries of the old British railway companies: maroon for the London, Midland and Scottish (LMS); brown and cream for the Great Western Railway (GWR); green for the Southern Railway (SR); and blue for the London and North Eastern Railway (LNER). c.1938; "Horse" and trailer 4½in long.* The set **£400–£600**

▷ **MOTORBIKE AND SIDECAR** *made in the U.S. by the Tootsietoy company. The figures are police officers, and details of the motorbike's construction, even down to the drum brake on the front wheel, are closely observed. 1920s; 5in long.* **£15–£25**

DINKY TOYS
178
WITH WINDOWS
PLYMOUTH PLAZA

▽ **DINKY SUPERTOY LORRIES**
The perennial popularity of models of commercial vehicles of all types is reflected by this lorry, bearing the name of J. Lyons & Co., and the eight-wheeled, 14-ton Foden tanker. c.1955; Tanker 7¾in long. **Lyons lorry £400–£600; Foden tanker £100–£150**

△ **DINKY PLYMOUTH PLAZA**
This model of an American sports car (shown with its original box) was in production until 1963. c.1959; 4½in long. **£30–£40**

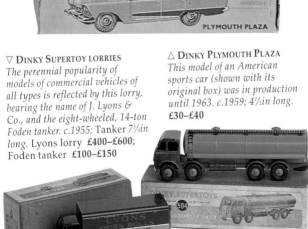

Dinky introduced a range of slightly larger models in 1948 known as Supertoys, into which most of the lorries and vans fell. As with the original Dinky Toys, it was the remarkable attention to detail and the high quality of the painting that put these vehicles ahead of most of the competition.

Since fewer models of the Supertoys were made than of the smaller range, some of these vehicles, for instance, eight-wheeled Foden lorries, are extremely rare and can command prices of £300–£400 when boxed and in good condition.

DATING DINKY TOYS
The following pointers give a general guide to dating, although there are exceptions.

Prewar Features
1 Plain metal wheel hubs.
2 Silver plating on wheels.
3 White tyres.
4 No model name and/or number on either the base plate or chassis.
5 Wing-mounted spare wheels.
6 Cars and lorries are boxed in sets, never individually.

Postwar Developments
1 Wheel hubs have a raised circle resembling a hubcap.
2 All models bear both a name and a number.
3 Dinky Supertoys were made only from 1947.
4 Windscreens from late 1950s.
5 Aluminium wheels date from 1959.
6 Opening doors and movable steering wheels etc. date from the early 1960s.

▷ **THREE DIE-CAST DINKY TOYS** *which are in excellent condition. The Foden flat truck is 8 inches long; the open-*

◁ **DINKY SUPERTOY TURNTABLE FIRE ESCAPE LORRIES** *such as these were first issued in 1958. The great discrepancy in the price of these two identical lorries demonstrates the importance to collectors of the condition of die-cast toys and the existence of the original box. c.1960; 6in long.*
Mint model **£150–£200**
Battered model **£2–£3**

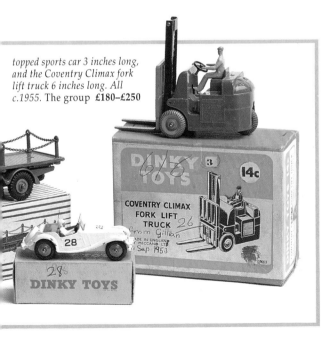

topped sports car 3 inches long, and the Coventry Climax fork lift truck 6 inches long. All c.1955. The group **£180–£250**

After World War II, Dinky was challenged by other makers, notably Lesney, who in 1953 began to produce its Matchbox Miniatures – toys so tiny that they could often fit into a matchbox. These were mostly contemporary vehicles, but in 1956 Lesney launched the Models of Yesteryear range of larger classic vehicles and trains.

In the same year, the Mettoy company produced the innovative Corgi range of slightly larger vehicles, with windows, independent suspension and bonnets that could be opened to reveal the engine.

▽ **Matchbox removals van**
This flat-topped model, which was reissued in 1958 with a curved roof, was available in three other colours. c.1956; 2in long. **£35–£40**

△ **Early Matchbox cars** *were distributed by Moko. Generally speaking, boxed vehicles are the most valuable, but here, the two-tone Vauxhall Cresta, although it*

△ **CORGI MGA** *The white-walled tyres on this die-cast sports car, with aluminium-painted hubcaps, are not accurate; they should be black. The car was also available with a cream or white body. c.1957; 4in long.* **£40–60**

no longer has its original box, is the most sought-after model. 1950s; all vehicles 2in long. **£30–40**

▽ **MATCHBOX "BROOKE BOND" TEA VAN** *Advertising on toy commercial vehicles, which proved popular with children, was first used in Britain by Hornby. 1950s; 2in long.* **£35–40**

MODEL RAILWAYS

The first toy trains were made in the 1830s of either metal or wood and were pulled along the floor. It was not until later in the century that they were designed to run on tracks. By 1900, clockwork trains were common and the first electric sets had been invented.

Before World War I, the European market was dominated by German manufacturers such as Märklin, Bing and Carette. After the war, however, the field became more open. The English firm Bassett Lowke, which had distributed some of the German firms' products alongside its own, became more independent, and Hornby launched its first train set. In America, the important manufacturers were Ives, Lionel and American Flyer.

▽ PART OF A HORNBY TRAIN SET
with the original box behind. These clockwork O-gauge goods wagons are in excellent condition, which increases their value. c.1926; Large wagon *9in long.* **£100–£125**

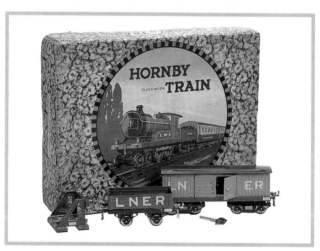

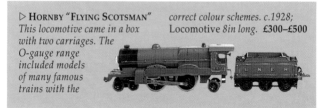

▷ HORNBY "FLYING SCOTSMAN"
This locomotive came in a box with two carriages. The O-gauge range included models of many famous trains with the correct colour schemes. c.1928; Locomotive *8in long.* **£300–£500**

△ **RARE ELECTRIC TRAIN SET**
Made by Ever Ready, this unusual battery-operated train set was part of a short-lived attempt by the battery makers to break into the toy *market. It is actually an underground train set with 1938 stock of London's Bakerloo tube line. When new it cost £3. 6s. 9d. c.1948; Train 8in long.* **£100–£150**

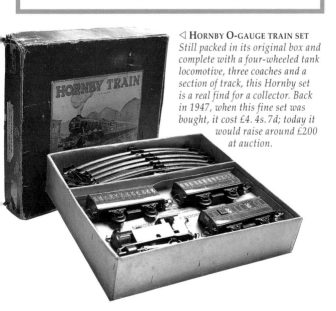

◁ **HORNBY O-GAUGE TRAIN SET**
Still packed in its original box and complete with a four-wheeled tank locomotive, three coaches and a section of track, this Hornby set is a real find for a collector. Back in 1947, when this fine set was bought, it cost £4. 4s. 7d; today it would raise around £200 at auction.

Frank Hornby, the inventor of Meccano, was also one of the most influential model railway makers. In 1920, he launched his first train set with a simple clockwork tin train. His trains fitted track 1¼ inches apart, which was known as O gauge.

Over the next decades the variety of the toys increased and Hornby catalogues showed locomotives, tenders, carriages and accessories in a number of liveries. During 1925, Hornby produced its first electric train. It used the three-rail system, with an electrified central rail, and soon became popular.

The Dublo gauge, half the size of O gauge, was introduced in 1938. This range became famous around the world for the accuracy of detail, achieved using the die-casting technique, and the variety of locomotives, rolling stock and accessories.

△ **ELECTRIC LOCOMOTIVE**
Although this class 81 electric locomotive was made recently and so is relatively cheap to buy, its value will increase over the years making it a good potential purchase for new collectors. 1960s; 9in long.

▷ **"SIR NIGEL GRESLEY"** *was the first model in the Dublo range introduced by Hornby in 1938 and it remains one of the most popular Dublo models. Pre-World War II examples can be identified by the deeper valance over the wheels. c.1950; 11in long.* **£150–£250**

▷ **THREE-RAIL ELECTRIC TRAIN**
Produced by Meccano, this goods train was part of the Hornby Dublo range. The middle rail of three-rail track was live and made electrical contact with a pick-up on the underside of the locomotive.

In 1938, Dublo, or OO, gauge was introduced to suit smaller houses. The width between the tracks was ⅝ inch, half that of the standard O gauge. c.1950; Engine 6in long. The group **£60–£80**

HORNBY "PRINCESS ELIZABETH" LOCOMOTIVE

Probably the best-known model locomotive, the "Princess Elizabeth" was made in vast numbers. This 11-inch model, the Dublo version featuring the green livery of British Rail, was first issued in 1952.

Hornby released several versions of this locomotive. The most valuable is the larger O-gauge three-rail electric model launched in 1938 and decorated in the maroon livery of the London, Midland & Scottish Railway (LMS). Made in limited numbers, a boxed set in mint condition could fetch as much as £2,000.

This Dublo example dates from about 1958. **£60–£80**

CONSTRUCTION SETS

The first toys to be produced as construction kits were designed by Frank Hornby and based on gadgets he made for his sons. His first commercial toy, "Mechanics Made Easy", was a boxed collection of pierced metal components from which an endless variety of machines could be made. These sets, now rare, were renamed "Meccano" in 1907 and remained popular for more than 60 years.

Although successful, these kits did not produce lifelike cars or aeroplanes, which led Hornby in 1931 to introduce a range of constructor sets. With a simple nut and bolt assembly, beautiful toys could be built. These kits remained in production until World War II.

▽ **MECCANO SET** *complete with its original wooden box. This kit, no. 7, was the most comprehensive set available in the 1920s. Its range of plates, bolts and pulleys allowed complex pieces such as a loom to be built. c.1926; 26in wide.* **£600–£800**

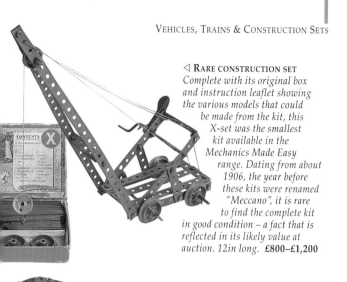

◁ **RARE CONSTRUCTION SET**
*Complete with its original box
and instruction leaflet showing
the various models that could
be made from the kit, this
X-set was the smallest
kit available in the
Mechanics Made Easy
range. Dating from about
1906, the year before
these kits were renamed
"Meccano", it is rare
to find the complete kit
in good condition – a fact that is
reflected in its likely value at
auction. 12in long.* **£800–£1,200**

△ **"BLUEBIRD"**
*Made from Meccano, this model
is of Sir Malcolm Campbell's car,
"Bluebird", in which he repeatedly
broke the land-speed record during
the 1930s – most famously in 1935.
Streamlined models, such as this,
were only possible once flexible
metal construction plates had been
introduced, also in the 1930s.
c.1939; 22in long.* **£150–£200**

▷ **MECCANO SET NO. 7**
*In 1945, Meccano introduced
its famous red and green colour
scheme which remained in use
until the 1960s. Although this
set is in pristine condition, it is
much later than the other example
of set no. 7 featured here (above
left), hence the lower valuation.
c.1948; 19in wide.* **£150–£200**

GAMES

The appeal of games for
enthusiasts must lie partly in nostalgia
for childhood and partly in a delight
in the colourful diversity and
novelty of these toys.
The earliest commercially produced
board games were intended as
educational or moral aids for children,
but by the mid-19th century and early
20th century children played
games for fun alone.
At their most fascinating, board games
reflect the preoccupations of each age,
with subjects as diverse as military
battles, horse racing and space travel.
Others are bright new variations
of such age-old favourites as ludo
and snakes and ladders. Good examples
of collectable games can be bought for a
few pounds, while the most decorative
carved chess sets can command
thousands. Condition is all-important:
the most valuable games are those
that are undamaged and in the
maker's original box.

BOARD & OTHER GAMES

For over 5,000 years, board games have been played in all cultures. Traditional themes of confrontation, competition and chance still dominate new games today. Chess is one of the earliest "war" games, though the style of the pieces is medieval.

Victorian times saw a great expansion in board games, when favourites such as ludo and snakes and ladders emerged in the form children know today. The famous 20th-century game is Monopoly, which dates from the 1930s. Early sets can fetch hundreds of pounds.

The period feel of some games such as Cluedo and Dover Patrol, with its Dreadnought battle fleets, has a special appeal for collectors. Condition is all-important in assessing a board game's value, and many collectors never play their own games because of this.

△ **VICTORIAN GAMES COMPENDIUM**
Attractive set in mint condition containing both board and card games. The box is mounted with brass and inlaid with pietra dura *(semiprecious stone) plaques. Inside are ivory pieces for chess and backgammon, boards for* cribbage and bridge, dice and turned wood shakers. Counters, shakers and cards are kept in the lower drawer (shown open here). c.1870; 14in wide. **£1,200–£1,500**

◁ **ELECTRIC ROULETTE GAME** *made by Chad Valley. There are five coloured compartments in the box lid on which to bet. The wheel is spun and a metal ball drops through one of the holes around the tray causing a bulb to light in the winning compartment.* c.1928; 14in x 10in. **£25–£30**

△ **BONE AND BAMBOO MAHJONG SET** *in a wooden box. In this Chinese game, players try to win hands with combinations of tiles.* 1920s; box 10in x 6in. **£70–£100**

▽ **"THE INVASION OF EUROPE"** *A rare war game made by Chad Valley. Two rival invasion forces, one naval and one military, try to reach the ringed cities using dice and a compass (missing from this set).* c.1910; 24in long. **£80–£120**

△ **"MOTOR CHASE ACROSS LONDON"** *Geographica Ltd specialized in race games involving maps of Britain.* 1930s; 20in long. **£40–£60**

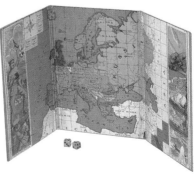

△ **VICTORIAN CHESS SET** *The box, made from moulded composition on a cardboard support, is in the shape of a fortress, decorated with royal and courtly figures. It contains lead-weighted ebony and boxwood chessmen made by Jacques Staunton, the most celebrated designer of chess pieces. 1880s; 7in wide.* **£800–£1,000**

▷ **CHESS SET** *with large English barleycorn-pattern chessmen made of bone probably in India; one side is stained red. The overall quality is excellent and only the knights have needed repair. The fitted case is constructed of mahogany and is lined with velvet ribbon. 1825–50; 5½in wide.* **£400–£600**

◁ **CHINESE CHESS SET** *This high-quality set originates from Macau in southeast China. The chessmen are deeply carved and the set is complete with draughtsmen, dice and shakers. The box is of ivory inlaid in a form of pictorial marquetry known as intarsia. c.1860; 17in wide.* **£1,000–£1,500**

△ **"PHYSOGS"** *An English game made by Waddy. Players are dealt a word that corresponds to a facial expression, such as "stubborn", and must accumulate cards, depicting eyes, nose, mouth and so on, which make up that expression when assembled. The winner is the player who comes closest to the ideal set by the makers of the game. 1930s; 14in x 10in.* **£30–£40**

▷ **TABLE-TOP HORSE RACING GAME** *made by Ayers and Co., makers of billiard tables. Based on roulette, it consists of a wheel with divisions that correspond to race horses with different odds. Bets are placed on the baize cloth before the "race", when the wheel is spun. c.1880; 5ft 8in long.* **£1,500–£1,800**

◁ **GERMAN SKITTLES SET** *comprising three geisha girls, three pug dogs (one with a crown), three tabby cats and a wooden ball. The skittles on turned wood bases are made of printed cloth, with metal-thread embroidery. c.1870; cat 7in high.* **£400–£500**

COLLECTOR'S CHECKLIST

PEOPLE ARE INSPIRED TO COLLECT toys and games for many different reasons: to form a collection or own a great rarity, for example, or even to acquire a plaything desired since childhood.

Movable models of human figures date back to the time of the Egyptians but, in collecting terms, the most desirable of the early dolls are the wooden ones that date from the 1600s. They are carved, covered in gesso (plaster mixed with size) and painted, and are often exquisitely dressed in contemporary costume. The best examples, in original condition, can fetch more than £30,000.

At the other end of the scale are the fabric and soft dolls made from the late 19th century. Fabric and rag dolls by companies such as Steiff, Lenci, Käthe Kruse, Norah Wellings and Dean's Rag Book Co. have become more popular over the last few years, with some examples made as recently as 1925 realizing more than £1,000.

The market for teddy bears has been buoyant for several years, but today all sorts of soft toys are enthusiastically collected, either by maker (such as Steiff, Dean's Rag Book Co., Merrythought or Schuco) or by type. Cartoon characters such as Mickey and Minnie Mouse, Donald Duck, Snow White and the Seven Dwarfs, Oswald Rabbit and Dismal Desmond are all popular.

The trains, boats and vehicles made from tin plate in the "Golden Age" of toy making, between 1900 and 1914, are most highly regarded in collecting circles, especially if they are by the best German manufacturers: Märklin, Bing, Gunthermann and Carette. Expensive when produced, these toys were the playthings of wealthy children; today the same toys can fetch tens of thousands of pounds if they are rare and in good condition.

Some collectors look for more modern battery-operated toys, including novelty figures, robots and space toys; and cars from the 1950s are extremely popular today. Toys that were made following the success of a film or television series, for example *Batman, Thunderbirds* or the James Bond films, have risen rapidly in price recently.

Condition is increasingly important with toys of this vintage, since collectors will only pay high prices for items in near mint condition with, if possible, their original boxes.

For many years, children's non-mechanical games and educational amusements were not as widely collected as clockwork toys, but there has been a great surge of interest, particularly in America, which has begun to affect prices in Europe.

The demand for board games, puzzles and educational toys reflects this new awareness, while the publication of specialist books has triggered wider interest in, for instance, pedal cars and rocking horses.

The number of collectors of toys and games continues to grow, and today the market thrives internationally, with regular auctions, fairs and exhibitions dedicated to the playthings from times past.

As with any other collectable, the best prices are achieved by items that have not undergone amateur restoration.

TIPS FOR BUYERS

1 Look at the back of a bisque doll's head for the maker's marks and the mould number. These enable the doll to be identified and valued.

2 Check the heads and limbs of china and bisque dolls for cracks or chips, since even a hairline crack will dramatically affect the value of the doll.

3 Look in the left ear of a soft doll or animal; if a small embossed metal rivet pierces the ear, it is likely to be a highly collectable product of the German manufacturer Steiff.

4 Check whether teddy bears or soft toys have been patched, darned or resewn – such repairs will adversely affect a toy's value.

5 Recently made dolls' prams have been imported into Europe from the Far East in vast numbers. Once "aged", they are difficult to tell from Victorian originals.

6 Many cast-iron mechanical money banks were copied and reproduced in Taiwan in the 1970s; these are worthless to collectors.

7 Check Hornby trains from the 1930s or Dinky Toys for metal fatigue. The alloy on some of these is prone to flaking and crumbling.

8 Don't buy rusty tin-plate toys. If they are badly affected, the decoration (and the toy) is likely to be unrestorable.

9 Playthings are worth more with their original boxes, but don't try to repair a damaged box yourself.

10 To be of interest to collectors, board games must be complete with their original playing pieces, dice and instructions.

SOME TOY AND DOLL MUSEUMS
Anglesey Museum of Childhood
1 Castle Street, Beaumaris
Gwynedd LL58 8AP
Telephone: 01248 810 448
Arundel Toy and Military Museum
23 High Street, Arundel
West Sussex BN18 9AD
Telephone: 01903 882 908
Bethnal Green Museum of Childhood
Cambridge Heath Road
London E2 9PA
Telephone: 0181 980 2415
Chester Toy & Doll Museum
13A Lower Bridge Street Row
Chester CH1 1RS
Telephone: 01244 346297
Haworth Museum of Childhood
117 Main Street, Haworth
Keighley, W Yorkshire BD22 8DP
Telephone: 01535 643593
Museum of Childhood Edinburgh
42 High Street (Royal Mile)
Edinburgh EH1 1TG
Telephone: 0131 225 2424
Ribchester Museum of Childhood
Church Street, Ribchester
Lancashire PR3 3YE
Telephone: 01254 878520

Caring for your Valuables

Antiques may be bought for their beauty, craftsmanship, history, rarity or even for their curiosity value. It does not matter whether you buy an item because it gives you pleasure, or because you consider it to be a serious investment: it is important to see that it is well looked after and properly insured. That way, it can be enjoyed today and handed down from generation to generation.

Furniture

If you own any pieces of antique furniture, remember that they also require care and, often, repair. However, if you are planning to sell a piece, it is often better to leave it in its original condition, since collectors sometimes prefer to have repairs done themselves.

In almost all instances, it is unwise to try to restore furniture yourself. Poor-quality repairs often reduce value considerably; more importantly, they can cause irreversible damage. Experts always advise owners to seek out a first-class repairer or restorer. Even if their charges are high, it is cost-effective to pay a higher price for excellent work.

After you have used furniture for many years, it is wise to have it checked over by a skilled repairer and to have loose joints or flaking veneers fixed – before you pass it on to your heirs!

Caring for furniture

1 The most important thing about looking after antique furniture is to remember that "gently does it". It is very easy to remove patina and colour but impossible to replace them. Light dusting with a soft cloth and occasional cleaning and polishing are all that is needed.

2 The safest way to clean antique furniture is to apply a little clear wax with a soft shoe brush, rub vigorously, then buff it with a soft cloth. If more cleaning is needed, consult an expert. Good-quality furniture will already have been treated with grain filler and surface polish, so little further attention is required.

3 Never strip the surface of a piece of furniture. For instance, with some wax polishes the instructions for use recommend application with wire wool. Never do this: the combination of wax and wire wool will undo the patina that has been acquired over generations in two or three strokes.

4 Don't use "traditional" remedies, such as lemon juice, olive oil or methylated spirit, and avoid patent cleaning mixtures.

5 If stains have been made by plant pots, flower vases or glasses, do not apply anything to the mark until it is properly dry – at least two weeks. It is worth being patient because in most instances the black stain will disappear of its own accord. The application of any "remedy" may mean that the scar becomes permanent.

6 Wooden furniture should not stand in direct sunlight; prolonged exposure will bleach out the colour. Nor should it be placed close to a heat source, such as a radiator, hot air duct, electric or open fire. This will cause the wood to dry out and crack, veneers and inlays to shrink and warp and joints to open up. Keep the air moist by standing a bowl of water near the heat source or by installing a humidifier.

7 Don't polish gilded or brass handles. If the gilding has worn away, the handle underneath should appear bronze coloured.

8 Ormolu mounts should be dusted gently with a soft brush but should never be polished, even with a dry cloth. Never have faded ormolu regilded; this may detract from the value of the piece.

9 Take expert advice before changing upholstery. Reupholstery should be carried out using traditional materials, such as canvas webbing and horsehair

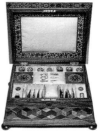

padding, not foam rubber. Fabric should be secured with tacks, not a staple gun.

10 Upholstered furniture can be carefully vacuumed; secure a cloth over the nozzle of the vacuum cleaner if the upholstery is worn.

11 Make sure that the seat is returned to its original chair when drop-in seats are reupholstered. The shape of seats varies marginally and the incorrect seat can put a strain on chair joints.

12 Have an expert repair chipped gilding. Chips can be filled and painted to match, but this is not a job for the amateur.

13 Furniture should be inspected at least twice a year for woodworm, and if tiny holes and fresh sawdust are found, it should be treated with woodworm fluid.

CERAMICS

One of the chief joys of collecting antique ceramics must be that most wares were made for a practical purpose, and there is no reason why a careful owner should not continue to use them in the same way. How much more memorable to serve tea from an antique tea set or to hold a dinner party at which your guests dine from century-old plates.

Similarly, it is perfectly acceptable to display cut flowers in an antique vase, provided the water is held in a separate container to prevent staining. Earthenware and ceramics with a crazed glaze, such as bone china and some soft-paste porcelain, are water permeable, while hard-paste porcelain and stoneware are not.

More delicate pieces should be kept only for display on secure shelves or in cabinets, preferably locked. Take particular care with lids and areas that have been restored or are cracked.

CARING FOR CERAMICS

1 All antique ceramics should be washed by hand – never put them in a dishwasher.
2 When a plate or dish has been used for cheese or any other fatty food, wash it immediately. Oily substances are difficult, if not impossible, to remove once they have penetrated the body.
3 Do not immerse any earthenware with an unglazed foot rim or cracks, since moisture will be absorbed and may discolour the piece. It is safer to wipe it with a cloth dipped in warm water containing a little mild detergent.
4 Use a shower attachment when washing flower-encrusted and other delicate items, then leave them to dry. If you dry such pieces with a tea towel, you run the risk of its snagging and breaking off pieces of the porcelain.

5 Do not handle unglazed pottery with unclean hands. Greasy fingers may mark permanently.
6 Do not use household bleach or a cleaner containing chlorine. If hard- or soft-paste porcelain is discoloured, the staining can sometimes be removed by using a 20 percent solution of hydrogen peroxide, available from chemists,

combined with a few drops of ammonia. Wear rubber gloves and dip strips of cottonwool in the solution. Lay them on the stain for about an hour, but do not let them dry on the surface. Repeat if the stain has not disappeared. This treatment is not suitable for pieces with any gilding or lustre decoration or with pale blue or greenish, 19th-century enamelling.
7 Do not warm porcelain plates and tureens in the oven, even at the coolest setting, since the glaze may craze. Heat them by placing them in hot water for a minute or two, then dry carefully.
8 Always hold cups, mugs, jugs and teapots by the body, with the base supported, never by the handle alone.
9 When hanging plates on the wall, always use the plastic-coated plate hangers that can be adjusted to fit individual plates; they are available from all good china shops. Stick-on plate hangers may remove the glaze from delft and majolica. Never hang cracked

plates on the wall.

10 Good pieces of pottery or porcelain should only be repaired or restored by professionals. If an item is broken, collect all the pieces, even the tiniest, wrap them in paper and take them to a professional restorer.

11 Unless you want to sell a piece, do not have it restored or any damage repaired, unless it offends you.

12 When moving ceramics, never pack them in tea towels or fabric of any kind in case the material snags and damages the pieces. Use bubblewrap or newspaper. Pack plates vertically, do not stack them one on top of the other.

CLOCKS AND WATCHES

When taking care of antique clocks you must remember that they are working mechanisms and need regular attention in order to keep them running. If you neglect your clocks, repairs may be expensive. Always seek out a first-class repairer or restorer;

even if it seems rather expensive, it is still cost-effective to pay for excellent work by knowledgeable people.

Even if a clock or watch is in perfect working order, it should still be serviced regularly: about once every ten years would be appropriate for sturdy movements

such as those found in longcase clocks; once every five years for more delicate ones.

Clocks can be harmed irrevocably by being left in an poor position. They should never be exposed to extremes of heat or light. Therefore, you should not leave a clock on a mantelpiece above a working fire. When a suitable position has been found, long-case and wall-mounted clocks should be firmly secured by their brackets, with the base plate absolutely horizontal. Clocks must be handled with care and held upright by the main part of the case only – never by any external parts. If the pendulum is a suspended one, it should be fastened; a clip or screw clamp is often provided for this purpose. If not, the pendulum must be removed. The weights and pendulum of a longcase clock should always be unhooked when the clock is moved, and the movement taken out of the case. Only the correct, undamaged key should be used to open the case.

It is never advisable to run any clock for long periods when the movement is dirty. Longcase clocks, however, are forgiving, and a properly adjusted longcase movement will run for years, even if slightly neglected.

If the mechanism is left to run down completely, clocks can be harmed; for this reason, they should always be stopped before any protracted absence.

When moving the hands, touch the minute hand by the base only, never at the tip, to avoid breaking it. Obstructions should never be forced; try to find the cause of the blockage first and if this is not possible, seek expert help. The hour hand of a striking clock should never be moved anti-clockwise beyond the "twelve". (There is no danger of moving the hour hand of a simple, non-striking timepiece, however.) If a striking clock shows the incorrect time, it is advisable to stop the movement so that the hour hand need be moved on only slightly.

Do not open the back of a watch with a knife. Repairs to both wrist and pocket watches should always be left to specialists.

If a movement is in good condition, or can be cleaned for a reasonable price, a little home "surgery" can often refresh the case. The following general rules should be strictly observed.

CARING FOR CLOCKS AND WATCHES

1 To improve wooden clock cases that have become dull, try a good wax polish; if this is unsuccessful use a proprietary surface cleaner. To remove stubborn surface grime, the cleaner may be used with 0000 grade wire wool.

2 Wood, marble or stone cases that have come apart should be

reassembled with water-soluble adhesive. (Never use impact or contact adhesives, which are impossible to remove.)

3 Clean marble clocks by wiping them gently with a cloth that has been dampened with water and a mild solution of washing-up liquid. Remove any grease from the case with some cottonwool soaked in benzine and wipe the surface dry immediately.

4 To improve dulled black marble, apply several thin coats of black shoe polish.

5 Be careful when attempting to clean metal cases. Brass may be

cleaned with non-abrasive metal polish, but gilded metals need specialist treatment. Bronze should not be polished, simply dusted occasionally.

6 Never oil a dirty clock. If you are cleaning the movement, make sure it is completely unwound before dismantling. Thoroughly wash the parts using benzine and clean the pivot holes with sharpened matchsticks. When re-assembling the clock, put a drop of light oil, such as sewing-machine oil, on each pivot and on the pallets of the escapement, but do not oil the wheels.

DOLLS AND TOYS

As with any other collectable, precious dolls and toys require care and, sometimes, repair. However, in many cases, it is

better to leave soft toys in their original condition if you think you might like to sell them.

Bear in mind, also, that the best prices are achieved by pieces that have not undergone amateur restoration. Poor-quality work often reduces the value and can cause irreversible damage.

Once your treasures are in good condition, keep them that way by following these tips.

CARING FOR TOYS

1 Keep dolls in a clean, dustproof box or case with by acid-free tissue or card and away from any heat source. If the doll is stuffed with hair or wool, add a few mothballs from time to time, but do not let them touch the doll or its clothes.

2 Wooden dolls with gesso or varnished faces and limbs should never be cleaned with water, since both these are water soluble. The same applies to composition dolls. Both types can be cleaned with a soft brush or by rubbing with soft white bread.

3 Never try to clean or repair a wax doll; leave it to an expert.

4 Clean the faces of bisque or china dolls by wiping them with damp cottonwool and a little soap. Wipe with another piece of damp cottonwool to remove the soap and dirt. Take care not to get the head or wig wet. Allow them to dry naturally.

5 Dolls sometimes need new wigs; do not use elaborate wigs made from nylon. Look at similar dolls to your own before deciding on a style. Replacement wigs can be expensive and hard to find. A new wig should be pasted on with a water-soluble glue.

6 Restringing detached limbs or restitching cloth or kid bodies, is best left to an expert.

7 Original clothing can enhance the value of a doll, but it needs to be treated with care. Any cleaning or mending is best done by an expert. Cloth is weakened every time it is cleaned, so don't clean it too often; never iron dirty fabrics, since heat may cause fading, fix stains and seal dust into the cloth.

8 Teddy bears, soft toys and rag dolls can be brushed and gently vacuumed to remove surface dirt. Occasionally they should be sealed in a plastic bag with insecticide pellets to prevent infestation by moths and other pests – but only if children are not going to play with the toy.

9 Dust tin-plate, brass, lead, cast-iron and die-cast toys gently with a soft brush or cloth. Remove any ingrained dirt with a non-abrasive silicone polish on a soft cloth. (Try it out on an unexposed part first.)

10 Never use abrasive cleaners on these toys, or polishes designed to revive the colour of full-size motor cars.

11 Don't repaint die-cast cars, for

this will greatly lower their value.

12 Take batteries out of battery-driven toys when they are stored.

13 Oil moving parts of a clock-work mechanism with a drop of light oil. Wipe off any excess.

14 Where possible, save original boxes, but don't attempt to repair them yourself.

15 Check wooden toys such as dolls' houses, Noah's arks and rocking horses for woodworm periodically. Treat them if necessary.

16 Don't keep china dolls on a narrow, flimsy shelf or wax dolls too close to a source of heat or where the sun will shine on them. If they get too warm, their eyes may protrude and the chemicals in their colouring may become purplish. Varnished dolls tend to yellow with age, and this will be accelerated by heat.

17 Don't keep toys and games directly under a water tank or bathroom.

INSURANCE

Insurance cover varies greatly. Cover for valuable antiques can be expensive, but the lowest quotation is not always the best one. Specialist brokers, as well as building society insurance services, understand collectors' needs.

Decide on the kind of "risks" that you want covered. Comprehensive and All In policies cover only certain specified perils, such as theft, fire, explosion, water or storm damage. In the event of theft, you must notify the police and provide evidence.

All Risks is the maximum cover and also covers accidental breakage and disappearance, but not "inherent vice", such as the progressive deterioration of cloth-bodied dolls, for example.

List the items you wish to insure with as much detail as possible. It is advisable to keep receipts as back-up evidence if you have to make a claim. Insurance companies also sometimes ask to see photographs, credit card vouchers or notes of any distinguishing marks.

You may even need to consider a policy that covers your possessions away from home, such as when they are sent to restorers or if you are selling them at an antiques fair.

If you want a valuation get two quotes from reputable dealers or auction houses. (There may be a small fee.) Most insurance valuations are based on the full replacement cost of an item, which is why you should give your insurers as much detail as possible, including where you keep your collection and how you protect it.

If you under-insure, insurance companies are likely to scale down their pay-outs – or may even refuse to pay out at all. It is now

fairly standard practice not to pay a claim in cash, but to settle the claim once a replacement has been bought. Frequently you are expected to pay an "excess", which can be, for example, the first £25 of the cost of each claim.

Index-linked policies automatically adjust the amount of insurance cover, and your premiums, every year. Check the figures from time to time. It is a good idea to update valuations every few years because fantastic appreciation often occurs with certain periods or pieces.

Insurers are keen for you to take "reasonable" care of valuable items. Store them safely under good conditions.

It also makes sense to install smoke detectors, particularly in living areas, and to have fire extinguishers easily to hand.

If something does get broken or damaged, get the written approval of your insurance company before having it restored.

SECURITY

According to research, 1 in 12 households is burgled annually. But if you join a Neighbourhood Watch scheme the risk falls to 1 in 75, and it may also lower the cost

of your home contents premium. The local Crime Prevention Officer will be happy to help you set up a scheme if none exists. Usually you need half the people in your area – whether it is a street or block of flats – to agree to join.

Your Crime Prevention Officer should also be happy to advise on the adequacy of the locks and bolts that you have in your home. Security devices such as five-lever mortise locks on doors and key-operated window locks are fairly inexpensive to fit and highly effective; they may even help to reduce the cost of your premiums.

As a rule, two mortise dead-locks should be fitted to each external door, and window locks to all ground-floor and first-floor windows. Vulnerable windows, such as those in a basement, should have iron bars. Additional precautions, such as security bolts on doors, are worth considering, especially if a door is not made of timber or is less than 1¾ in thick.

Another way to deter burglars is to fit an alarm. This can also reduce your premiums, but don't go for the cheapest quote just to save a few pounds. You should choose a recognized organization that offers local maintenance facilities and a full guarantee. The local police or your insurers will probably be able to recommend appropriate companies to you.

If your home does get burgled, you should report the matter at the police station and to your insurers without delay.

GLOSSARY

Note: SMALL CAPITALS within an entry refer to another entry.

A

AESTHETIC MOVEMENT Decorative arts movement, much influenced by Oriental styles, which flourished in Britain and America c.1870–80.

APPLIED DECORATION A pre-prepared ornamental finish applied to a finished object.

APRON Shaped edging hanging below a drawer line or table top.

ARCHITECTURAL STYLE Term used to describe furniture and clock cases with features such as arches, pediments and columns.

ART DECO Style of art and decoration developed between 1918 and 1939, reflecting the machine age. First popularized at the 1925 Exposition des Arts Décoratifs in Paris, from which the term derives.

ARTS AND CRAFTS MOVEMENT Started in the late 1800s in Britain by a group of artists and craftsmen committed to handmade articles.

ASTRONOMICAL CLOCK Timepiece with a dial showing the phases of the moon and other phenomena.

B

BACK STOOL A stool with a back that later evolved into the side chair.

BACKBOARD The unpolished back of a piece of furniture.

BACKPLATE The plate behind a clock movement; one of two plates holding the mechanism in place. Plate behind a handle on a piece of furniture.

BALANCE SPRING Spring acting on the balance wheel in a watch mechanism to control the oscillations of the balance. Introduced to England by THOMAS TOMPION.

BALANCE WHEEL The wheel in a clock that controls the action of the ESCAPEMENT, thus regulating the movement.

BALUSTER Turned column with a curving shape, used for table legs and chair backs.

BANDING Decorative strips of inlay or veneer. Straight banding is cut with the grain; crossbanding is cut across it.

BANJO CLOCK Wall clock resembling an upturned banjo, first produced by the clockmakers Willard between 1780–1820 in Boston. Reproductions were common in the 19th C.

BAROQUE Heavily ornate style of architecture from late 17th-C Italy that influenced all the decorative arts throughout Europe c.1660–1730.

BASALT Black, fine-grained stoneware developed by several Staffordshire potters and improved by Josiah WEDGWOOD in the mid-1760s. This relatively cheap material was used to manufacture vases, copies of Classical bronzes and cameos.

BASSETT-LOWKE Model-toy company founded in Northampton in 1899 by W.J. Bassett-Lowke. Initially worked with BING and CARETTE. Established in its own right by the 1920s

BELLEEK Factory established in Northern Ireland in 1857. Specialized in woven parian PORCELAIN with motifs based on local flora and fauna. It also produced delicate, pearlized tableware.

BENTWOOD Lightweight or laminated timbers bent into curves by steaming or soaking in hot water.

BERLIN WOOLWORK Wool needlework depicting pastoral scenes, flowers or landscapes. Popular in Victorian era.

BEZEL A metal rim or setting that holds the glass on a clock or watch face in place.

BING Toy manufacturer founded by Adolf and Ignor Bing in the mid-1860s in Nuremberg. The firm made boats, clockwork figures, steam-driven models, trains and cars. Toys were marked GBN (Gebrüder Bing,

Nuremberg) until 1918 and BW (Bing Werke) after 1919. The Bing works closed in 1932.

BISCUIT POTTERY Ceramics that have been fired once but not glazed.

BISQUE AND COMPOSITION DOLLS Dolls with BISQUE heads and COMPOSITION bodies.

BISQUE Unglazed BISCUIT PORCELAIN used for dolls from the mid-19th C. After a first firing, the doll's features were painted on the face. The porcelain was refired at a low temperature.

BLANC-DE-CHINE Unpainted, highly translucent PORCELAIN made in Fujian Province, China, characterized by a thick glaze. Much copied in Europe in the 18th C.

BLOCK FRONT Front of a piece of furniture with two outward curves on either side of a central inward curve; common on American pieces.

BLUE AND WHITE Decorative scheme for pottery and PORCELAIN using COBALT BLUE as an underglaze.

BOBBIN TURNING Decoration on 17th- and 18th-C chair and table legs and stretchers, consisting of a series of wooden spheres turned on a lathe.

BODY The mixture of raw materials from which pottery or PORCELAIN is made. Often called "paste" when referring to porcelain.

BONE CHINA A hard, stable PORCELAIN made from bone ash and kaolin. Introduced by SPODE in 1794.

BOULLE A form of MARQUETRY using brass and tortoiseshell inlay, perfected in the 1700s by Louis XIV's cabinet maker André Charles Boulle.

BOW FRONT Curving, convex front on furniture such as chests of drawers.

BOW The largest 18th-C PORCELAIN factory in Britain, also known as New Canton. Founded in 1744 by Thomas Frye, it used soft-paste porcelain, invented in 1748, to make imitation Oriental porcelain and BLUE AND WHITE wares. Both figures and tablewares were made.

BRACKET FOOT Squared foot, usually used on 18th-C cabinet furniture.

BREGUET, ABRAHAM-LOUIS (1747–1823) A Swiss-born clock- and watchmaker living in Paris, who invented many features used in the modern watch.

BRITAIN, WILLIAM & SONS Founded in the mid-19th C in London, later moving to Birmingham. Originally made models, games and figures. Famous from 1893 for hollow-cast lead figures, especially lead soldiers; also farm and zoo sets and military items. In 1859 merged with Herald Miniature. W. Britains Ltd still exists.

BROCOT, ARCHILLE (1818–78) French clockmaker who, with his father Louis, invented the simple adjustable spring suspension for the pendulum.

BUN FOOT Style of rounded, slightly flattened foot on furniture, used from the late 17th C.

BURR WALNUT Wood cut from a cross-section of a gall or from the gnarled grain at the base of a tree; often used for VENEERS.

C

CABRIOLE Leg with a double curve: outward at the knee and inward above the foot.

CARETTE Company founded in Nuremberg in 1886 by Frenchman George Carette. One of the greatest toy manufacturers, it made high-quality, tin-plate toys. The large-scale boats, cars and trains were hand enamelled. Carette had links with both BING and BASSETT-LOWKE. It closed in 1917 and did not reopen until after the end of World War I.

CARTOUCHE DIAL A clock dial on which the numerals are painted on lozenge-shaped enamel plaques set within a decorative brass plate.

CASE FURNITURE A piece of furniture made to hold something.

CELLULOID A plastic used for dolls instead of BISQUE. The surface was painted a flesh-colour and then varnished.

CHAD VALLEY Company founded by Joseph and Alfred Johnson in 1860 in the Chad Valley, Birmingham. It moved to Harborne in 1897 and became known for well-made children's games. It developed "low-quality" tin-plate toys in the 30s and also made teddies and other soft toys. Between World War II and 1954 it produced DIE-CAST cars.

CHAMFER The angle on the edge of a piece of wood, achieved by planing or cutting.

CHAMPLEVÉ ENAMELLING Similar to cloisonné, whereby the cast-bronze body is cut away and filled with ENAMEL.

CHAPTER RING Circle on the dial of a clock or watch on which the hours are marked.

CHELSEA One of Britain's earliest PORCELAIN factories. Founded in 1745, it flourished until 1769 when it was sold to DERBY. It made luxury tablewares, tea sets and vases.

CHINOISERIE European imitations of Chinese decoration and design – in particular, fretwork, Oriental motifs and carving. Not to be confused with Chinese articles exported to Europe.

CHIP CARVING Pattern cut out of a wooden panel by chipping.

CHIPPENDALE, THOMAS (1718–79) English cabinet maker and designer, very influential in the mid-GEORGIAN period in England and the U.S.

CHRONOMETER Portable timepiece of great acccuracy developed in the 18th C to determine longitude at sea. Often mounted in a wooden box.

CLASSICAL STYLE 18th-C style much influenced by the arts and culture of ancient Greece and Rome.

CLAW AND BALL Foot shaped like a ball gripped by a claw. Used from c.1720, often with the CABRIOLE leg.

CLOBBERING Overpainting an existing design on ceramics with coloured ENAMELS or gilding. The Dutch often did this to Chinese BLUE AND WHITE.

COALPORT Shropshire-based PORCELAIN factory, established in 1795. Famous after 1810 for its smooth, translucent BONE CHINA. A maroon ground was introduced in

1821 and became a Coalport characteristic. Popular flower-encrusted ROCOCO vases and other pieces were produced in the 1830s. WEDGWOOD acquired the factory, which ceased production in 1926.

COBALT BLUE Pigment derived from cobalt oxide that could be fired at high temperature without changing colour; much used on early ceramics. Cf. BLUE AND WHITE

COCKBEADING Beaded MOULDING often used on drawer fronts.

CODEG Trademark for toys distributed by the British company Cowan de Groot, including the 1964 Dr Who Dalek (in both metal and plastic) and cheap tin-plate toys.

COMPOSITION Papier mâché or wood pulp and glue, used for dolls' bodies from the mid-C19 onward.

CREAMWARE Cheap, cream-coloured EARTHENWARE, made from Devon clay and ground burnt flints, with a transparent glaze. Refined in the 1760s by Josiah WEDGWOOD, it became known as "Queen's Ware", and became the standard domestic pottery used in Britain.

CYLINDER TOP Slatted or ridged curved lid that slides down from inside the top of a desk to cover the desktop.

D

DELFT Dutch centre for tin-glazed EARTHENWARE where, from the mid-16th C to the mid-18th C, potters adapted the designs on Chinese BLUE AND WHITE PORCELAIN. This largely domestic pottery was very successful until the emergence of CREAMWARE and PORCELAIN, which became freely available at the end of the 18th C.

DELFTWARE Tin-glazed pottery, made in England during the 17th C and 18th C, inspired by Dutch wares.

DERBY The first factory produced Meissen imitations in soft-paste PORCELAIN from 1750. In the 1770s, the Japanese IMARI style became strongly identified with Derby. In the early 19th C, BONE CHINA replaced soft-paste porcelain and Derby produced cheaper products until 1848, when it closed. The Crown Derby Porcelain Company was founded in 1876 to produce decorated and gilded bone china.

DIE-CASTING Process in which metal or plastic toys are cheaply produced from a reusable mould.

DINKY TOYS Range of toys produced from 1933 by MECCANO.

DOULTON Factory in Lambeth, London, founded by John Doulton (1793–1873), initially producing household stoneware. Doulton Studio art pottery was developed in the 1860s, influenced by the Lambeth School of Art. The factory also created Lambeth FAIENCE and silicon and MARQUETRY wares; in 1882, it launched high-quality PORCELAIN figures and tiles.

DOVETAIL Close-fitting joint with interlocking tenons. Used for drawers.

E

EARTHENWARE Porous pottery, fired at c.900–1,500°F, which is waterproof when glazed.

EAST, EDWARD Famous London clockmaker active mid-17th C; horologist to the court of Charles II.

EBONIZED WOOD Wood stained and polished to look like ebony.

ELASTOLIN Compound made from a mixture of sawdust, resin and glue, moulded around a wire structure. It was used by several German toy soldier manufacturers in the 1920s and '30s, but is extremely fragile.

ELLICOT, JOHN (1706–72) Master clockmaker to George III, who invented a form of compensated pendulum and improved the cylinder ESCAPEMENT.

ENAMEL A mixture of powdered glass and pigmented metallic oxides suspended in an oily medium, which can be fused to metal, glass or ceramics. The oily medium burns off during firing and the glass and oxides fuse to form a hard surface. White enamel was often used for clock and watch faces.

ENGRAVING Decoration in which lines or dots are incised into a hard surface, such as metal or glass, either with a steel or diamond tool or a spinning abrasive wheel.

ENTABLATURE An architectural term refering to the architrave, frieze and cornice that surmount columns on cabinets and clock-cases.

ESCAPEMENT Regulating mechanism of a clock that allows stored power in a falling weight or wound spring to be released at a regular rate.

ESCUTCHEON Decorative metal plate surrounding a keyhole.

F

FAIENCE French term for tin-glazed EARTHENWARE. See also DELFTWARE.

FAMILLE ROSE "Pink family"; opaque ENAMELS used on Chinese PORCELAIN from 1723 to 1735.

FAMILLE VERTE "Green family"; transparent green ENAMELS, used to decorate Chinese Kangxi-period (1661–1722) PORCELAIN.

FELDSPAR PORCELAIN BONE CHINA containing pure feldspar, rather than china stone,which is much tougher. First produced by COALPORT, but soon taken up by SPODE.

FINIAL Carved, turned or metal ornament on top of a piece of furniture.

FLAT CASTING Technique used since the early 18th C to produce small, thin figures. Pre-dates SOLID CASTING.

FOLIOT A horizontal rod with adjustable weights that regulated the verge ESCAPEMENT in the earliest clocks.

FRET PIERCING Fine decoration made by piercing the wood with a fret saw.

FRIEZE DRAWER Drawer in the frieze, or framework, just below a table top.

FROMANTEEL FAMILY Flemish family of clockmakers based in London in the 17th and early 18th C who made the first English pendulum clocks.

FUSEE Cone-shaped spool in a clock

around which gut or chain is wound in order to equalize the tension of the spring as it unwinds.

G

GALLERY Border around the top edge of a piece of furniture.
GEORGIAN British style roughly covering the reigns of George I (1714–27) to George III (1760–1820).
GESSO Plaster of paris.
GOTHIC Medieval style revived in the 18th and 19th C with pointed arches and pierced tracery.
GRAHAM, GEORGE (1673–1751) Invented the deadbeat ESCAPEMENT (1715) and mercury pendulum (1726), thus increasing the accuracy of longcase clocks. He also invented the cylinder escapement.
GRIDIRON PENDULUM A pendulum with alternating steel and brass rods that, despite changes in temperature, remains a constant length. It works because brass expands more slowly than steel so differences in the rates of expansion cancel each other out.
GUNTHERMANN Firm founded in 1877 in Nuremberg, famous for its well-made tin-plate fire engines, horse-drawn vehicles and planes.

H

HEPPLEWHITE, GEORGE (D.1786) English cabinet maker. An exponent of the NEO-CLASSICAL style, his useful designs are elegant and simple.
HOLLOW CASTING Process used for cheap tin toys in which molten alloy is poured into an engraved mould and then poured out again, leaving only the outer part to set. Patented in the 19 C by William BRITAIN.
HOOD The top of a longcase clock housing the movement and dial.
HOOPBACK CHAIR Chair where top rail and uprights form one curve.
HORNBY see MECCANO

I

IMARI WARE Japanese PORCELAIN, made at Arita from the 17th C, with panelled decoration drawn from local textile designs in underglaze blue, iron-red ENAMEL and gilding, and some black, green and yellow enamels. They inspired many 18th- and 19th-C European manufacturers, including DERBY and SPODE.
IMPRESSED MARK Pottery mark in which a row of letters or marks is stamped into the soft, unfired clay. Used on early pieces from BOW.
INCE AND MAYHEW Important mid-18th C English furniture makers.
INCISED MARK The earliest type of pottery mark in which a mark in scratched into the soft clay before firing; the edges often feel rough.

J

JAPANNING 18-C European technique using paint and varnish to imitate Oriental lacquerwork.
JAPONAISERIE European designs and forms influenced by Japanese style.
JUMEAU French doll maker. Gold medal (won at Paris exhibition in 1878) is often stamped on the body.

K

KAKIEMON WARE 17th-C Japanese PORCELAIN decorated with plants and birds in turquoise, vivid red, dark blue and black. Widely imitated in Europe in the 18th C.
KRAAK Chinese PORCELAIN, painted in underglaze blue, exported in the late 16th and early 17th C to Holland. The name comes from "carrack", the ship that transported it.

L

LACQUER Hard glossy resin from the tree *Rhus vernicifera* built up in several layers and then carved or inlaid with various materials.
LADY DOLLS "Adult" dolls dressed in the height of fashion. French lady dolls are often known as Parisiennes.
LEAD ALLOY An alloy of lead mixed with a cheaper metal such as tin.
LEHMANN One of the best makers of tin-plate novelty toys in the 1920s. Founded in 1881 in Brandenburg by Ernst Lehmann, the company moved

to West Germany near Nuremberg after 1945. It continued to produce tin-plate toys, some of which were based on its prewar classics.

LITHOGRAPHY Process that prints sheets of tin plate with decoration before they are pressed into shapes.

LOWBOY Small side table on CABRIOLE legs.

LUSTREWARE Pottery or PORCELAIN with a metallic glaze containing silver, copper, gold or platinum.

M

MAJOLICA Brightly decorated EARTHENWARE, moulded or pressed to produce a sharp relief. Developed by Herbert MINTON in 1851.

MÄRKLIN Set up at Goppingen, Germany, in 1859, Märklin made tin-plate vehicles, miniature furniture and novelty toys.

MARQUETRY Decorative VENEER on furniture in a pattern of naturalistic forms, such as shells or flowers.

MATCHBOX Miniatures Range of DIE-CAST models produced from 1953 by Lesney Products. Models were of contemporary vehicles such as the Morris Minor 1000 or Astin Martin DB2-4, Mark I.

MECCANO British toy company founded by Frank Hornby in 1901. Its first product was a construction kit (1908) and it went on to make clockwork, and later electric, trains and DIE-CAST vehicles and figures (which became the Dinky Toy range). In 1937 it launched OO-GAUGE train sets. Taken over in 1964 by Tri-ang, it closed down in 1979.

MERRYTHOUGHT Founded in 1930 by C. Randle and H. Janisch at Ironbridge, Shropshire. Best known for its teddy bears although it also made dolls, toys and games.

MINTON Factory established in 1793 by Thomas Minton, well known in the 19th C for MAJOLICA, parian and cloisonné work. It continues to produce high-quality PORCELAIN.

MOULDING Shaped strip of wood usually applied to the top of a piece of furniture, either as decoration or to conceal a joint.

MOVEMENT Mechanism of a clock or watch that causes it to work.

N

NEO-CLASSICISM Popular 18-C style using motifs inspired by the art and architecture of the Classical world.

NOMURA TOYS Founded in Tokyo in 1923, it produced a wide range of tin-plate clockwork novelty and character toys post 1945.

O-GAUGE 1¼-in track gauge used for early model railways.

OFFSET LITHOGRAPHY PROCESS see LITHOGRAPHY

OGEE Double curve, convex at the top and becoming concave at the bottom, often found on clock cases, MOULDINGS and on the feet of GEORGIAN furniture.

OO-GAUGE ⅝-inch track gauge, also known as Dublo, introduced by Frank Hornby in 1938 for MECCANO train sets to replace O-GAUGE.

ORMOLU Originally the powdered gold used to gild metal furniture mounts. The term now refers to the mounts themselves.

OYSTER VENEER VENEER made from vertical sections cut from walnut or laburnum branches, whose pattern resembles an oyster.

P, Q

PAD FOOT Simple end to a CABRIOLE leg, resting on a small disc, or pad.

PALLET The acting surfaces that alternately engage and release the escape wheel in a clock or watch movement.

PARISIENNE DOLLS see LADY DOLLS

PARQUETRY VENEER in geometric patterns, usually using laburnam OYSTER VENEER.

PEDIGREE London company mass-producing good-quality plastic dolls, including the Sindy Doll in 1963.

PEDIMENT Surmounts the cornice in cabinet furniture and longcase clocks. Fashions, such as the swan neck or broken arch, vary.

"PEG" DOLLS Simple, wooden, jointed dolls.

PETITE SONNERIE Striking mechanism that sounds ting-tangs every 15 minutes, and once on the hour.

PLANK Company active from 1866 in Nuremburg working in tin and brass. Famous for its steam-driven engines, ships, trains and cars.

PLATFORM ESCAPEMENT A complete clock ESCAPEMENT mounted on its own separate platform, notably used on carriage clocks.

PORCELAIN Mixture of china clay and china stone that becomes hard, translucent and white when fired. Hard-paste porcelain is fired at a higher temperature than soft paste and is cold to the touch. Soft paste is warmer with a softer glaze.

PUTTI Cupids or cherubs.

QUARE, Daniel (1647–1724) English clock- and barometer maker. The first to patent a REPEATER for watches.

R

REGENCY British decorative style named after George IV who ruled as regent for George III from 1811 to 1820 and as king until 1830.

REGULATOR A highly accurate pendulum clock, often used to set or check other timepieces.

REPEATER Clock or watch that, depending on its sophistication, repeats the previous hour, quarter hour and minutes when a cord or button is touched, thus telling the time without the face needing to be seen. First made in the 1680s.

REPOUSSÉ Term used in metalwork to describe a raised design created by hammering a thin sheet of metal. From the French for "pushed out".

ROCOCO Elaborate, curvilinear architectural style that originated in France in the early 18th C. Typical motifs include rocks, shells and floral designs.

S

SABRE LEG Sharply curved leg in the CLASSICAL style.

SCHUCO Trademark for German Company Schreyer & Co., founded in 1912, which made novelty clockwork toys in the 1920s and '30s. Post 1945 Schuco also produced a cheaper range of clockwork tin-plate cars. It closed in 1977, but sold its name to Gama, who remade several early Schuco models.

SCROLLWORK Curving decoration often found on clock cases.

SEAT BOARD Platform supporting the movement and face of a longcase clock.

SEAT RAIL Horizontal frame just below the seat of a chair that joins the chair legs.

SERPENTINE FRONT Sinuous double-curved front found on chest furniture, especially in the 18th C.

SHELF CLOCK Cheap clock developed in the U.S. to sit on a narrow shelf or ledge. Most have a plain rectangular frame and glass front.

SHERATON, THOMAS (1751–1806) English designer working in a light, delicate NEO-CLASSICAL style.

SHOULDER DOLL Doll that has its head and shoulders moulded in one piece (called a shoulder head).

SILK SUSPENSION MOVEMENT Pendulum suspended on a silk thread, found in most French 18th- and early 19th-C clocks.

SIMON & HALBIG PORCELAIN factory active in Thuringia from 1870. Made all-BISQUE dolls and bisque, COMPOSITION and CELLULOID heads.

SLIP Liquid clay, used to coat pottery, stick on external decoration or cast hollow figures.

SLIPWARE SLIP-decorated pottery.

SLIT-HEAD DOLLS Dolls whose hair is attached by means of small slits all over the head.

SOLID CASTING Technique used from the 19th C to produce three-dimensional toy figures.

SPLAT Central upright of a chair back, from the seat to the top rail.

SPODE Factory founded by Josiah Spode in 1770, initially producing domestic EARTHENWARE, including

CREAMWARE and TRANSFER-PRINTED Staffordshire blue, pioneered by Spode. After 1797 Spode produced BONE CHINA tableware and, from 1800, translucent FELDSPAR PORCELAIN using ENAMEL decoration in the REGENCY style. In 1846 the Spode factory, known as Copeland since 1833, perfected parian ware. It still continues to use the Spode trademark for its high-quality tablewares

SPRIGGING Ceramic decoration, shaped separately, then attached or "sprigged" with SLIP.

STAFFORDSHIRE POTTERIES British factories around Stoke-on-Trent, Burslem, Hanley, Tunstall, Longton and Fenton. Responsible for most innovations in ceramic techniques.

STEIFF Soft-toy company founded in the late 1870s in Grengen Brenz, Germany. Especially famous for its teddy bears.

STRETCHER Horizontal strut or rail bracing the legs of a chair or table.

STRINGING Fine strips of contrasting wood or metal inlaid in the wooden case of a clock or piece of furniture.

SUPERTOYS Large model vehicles produced by MECCANO.

T

TABERNACLE CLOCK 16th-C clock, often tower-shaped, sometimes with a dial on all four sides.

TIN PLATE A tin or tin-alloy coating or another metal – usually steel.

TOMPION, THOMAS (1638–1713) Famous English clockmaker who pioneered many inventions, including the BALANCE SPRING.

TOOTSIETOY Chicago-based toy company that specialized in DIE-CAST model vehicles. Its first models appeared in 1910, but its heyday was in the 1930s and '40s.

TRAIN The series of wheels in a clock or watch movement linking the power source (a weight or a spring) to a specific function, such as moving the hands or regulating the strike.

TRANSFER PRINTING Method of decorating mass-produced ceramics in which paper, printed with a design in metallic oxides, is wrapped round PORCELAIN and burnt away during firing, leaving the pattern. Invented in Britain in the mid-18th C, it is still the most common method of decoration in Europe and the U.S.

TWO-TRAIN MOVEMENT A movement with an extra function, either a striking, musical or alarm TRAIN. The first train moves the hands.

U, V

URN TABLE Small 18th-C table for holding a water urn or kettle.

VENEER Thin sheet of attractively grained wood (often walnut, satin- or rosewood) applied to a surface.

VERNIS MARTIN Form of LACQUER patented by Guillaume Martin and his brothers in the 18th C. Used for interior decoration and on small objects such as clock cases or boxes.

W

WAXED-COMPOSITION Doll's head or SHOULDER HEAD made of COMPOSITION covered with wax.

WEDGWOOD British pottery founded by Josiah Wedgwood (1730–95) in 1759 in Staffordshire. Reputation rests on innovations, designed to rival imported Chinese PORCELAIN, which included BASALT, CREAMWARE, pearlware and blue jasperware.

"WHITE" DIAL Painted metal clock face; often found after c.1775. Also known as a japanned dial.

WORCESTER British factory founded in 1751 and still active. Early on, it concentrated on soft-paste PORCELAIN decorated in underglaze blue and modelled on Meissen shapes. After 1763, it made copied Meissen, Sèvres and Japanese designs. BONE CHINA, introduced in 1800, was decorated by Chamberlains factory nearby; the two companies merged in 1840. In the 19 C, Worcester produced richly gilded and enamelled tablewares, figures, parian ware and Renaissance-style vases.

INDEX